MW01140917

Reading Matter

A Rabid Bibliophile's
Adventures Among
Old & Rare Books

In the privacy of our studies,
we embrace the world.

Reading Matter

A Rabid Bibliophile's Adventures Among Old & Rare Books

by

Jack Matthews

OAK KNOLL PRESS

New Castle, Delaware

2000

First Edition.

Published by **Oak Knoll Press**
310 Delaware Street, New Castle, Delaware, USA

Title: Reading Matter
Author: Jack Matthews
Typography: Nesbitt Graphics, Glenside, PA
Editor: Susan Rotondo
Photographer: Rick Fatica
Publishing Director: J. Lewis von Hoelle
Original Cover Art by: Barbara Matthews-Saunders

Copyright: © 2000 by Jack Matthews

Library of Congress Cataloging-in-Publication Data

Matthews, Jack.
    Reading matter : A rabid bibliophile's Adventures Among Old
and Rare Books / by Jack Matthews.—1st ed.
        p.   cm.
ISBN: 1-58456-027-4 (alk.paper)
    1. Matthews, Jack.   2. Book collectors—United States—
Biography.   3. Book collecting—United States.   4. Rare books—
Collectors and collecting.   I. Title.

Z989.M3 A3 2000
002'.075—dc21

                                                        00-031361

Printed in the United States of America on 60# archival, acid-free paper
meeting the requirements of the American Standard for Permanence of Paper
for Printed Library Materials.

Acknowledgements

I am pleased to acknowledge that some of the essays in this book first appeared in *The Antioch Review, Soundings,* and *The Washington Times*.

*This book is dedicated
to my Implied Readers,
most of whom are dead.*

Preface

*T*he title *Reading Matter* is clear enough, for with the exception of a small minority of illustrated books, what book isn't? But since all of the essays gathered here are directly or indirectly about collecting old and rare books, I intend a further meaning by the title, one that might help correct the stereotype of bibliophiles as mindless accumulators of "collectible" books, more interested in bibliographical niceties of edition, state and issue than in their contents, or "matter". . . and more interested in them as investments than as personal possessions.

But as great collectors have unanimously insisted throughout the ages, the richest and most meaningful sort of book collecting is that which is centered upon the mysterious beauty within the text—the story, the argument, the personal testimony from memory, the poetry, the exposition. In short, the book's reading matter matters, just as the title says.

I will also point out that some of the essays in *Reading Matter* are repetitious in their lyrical effusions over the delights in burrowing for the antiquarian lore in old books. These repetitions, however, serve a hortatory purpose—one which may, on the one hand, be dismissed as the rhetorical indulgence of a rabid enthusiast or, on the other, accepted as a just emphasis upon our abiding need for studying and understanding the Past by means of a passionate and civilized preoccupation with old and rare books.

I personally prefer the latter interpretation.

Books By Jack Matthews

FICTION
Bitter Knowledge
Hanger Stout Awake!
Beyond the Bridge
The Tale of Asa Bean
The Charisma Campaigns
Pictures of the Journey Back
Tales of the Ohio Land
Dubious Persuasions
Crazy Women
Sassafras
Ghostly Populations
Dirty Tricks
Storyhood As We Know It

POETRY
An Almanac For Twilight
Private Landscapes

NON-FICTION
Collecting Rare Books for Pleasure and Profit
Booking in the Heartland
Memoirs of a Bookman
Booking Pleasures
Reading Matter

PLAYS
On the Shore of That Beautiful Shore
An Interview with the Sphinx

Contents

List of Illustrations

FRONTISPIECE: In the Privacy of his Study, the Author Embraces the World.

Figure 1, page 1 (top): Glauber's 1670 book on alchemy, The Golden Ass, dressed handsomely in a modern binding.

Figure 2, page 1 (bottom): This copy of Trusler's 2 vol. 1833 edition of Hogarth is typical of the period's decorative bindings.

Figure 3, page 2: The magnificent 2 vol. "Pawnee Edition" of Washington Irving's *Captain Bonneville's Adventures* (NY, 1898), with and without dj.

Figure 4, page 3: Mark Twain's English first editions were handsomely bound in red cloth and are, of course, essential for any serious Mark Twain collection.

Figure 5, page 4: Theophilus Noel, sternly gazing out upon an imperfect world.

Figure 6, page 5: Pickering and Chatto's 1902 catalogue features this page from *Horae Beatae Mariae Virginis,* a French illuminated manuscript, circa 1480.

Figure 7, page 6: Also from the 1902 Pickering and Chatto catalogue is this illustration showing "Dr. Prosody in search of the Antique and Picturesque through Scotland, the Hebrides, the Orkney and Shetland Isles"

Figure 8, page 7 (top): *The Consort,* a rare instance of a book issued with two dustjackets (as shown), one within the other.

Figure 9, page 7 (bottom): Wendell Minor's dust jacket illustration for the author's novel, *Sassafras.*

Figure 10, page 8: Woodcut illustration from an imperfect copy of the rare 1808 edition of *The Western Pilot,* by Zadok Cramer.

Reading Matter

A Rabid Bibliophile's Adventures Among Old & Rare Books

1

Anecdotal Evidence

O ne can find both good news and bad news in the enduring popularity of trivia games. The good news is that such games trade upon real information—in contrast to, say, the brainless orgies of hysteria, vulgarity and canted rhetoric featured in the daytime game shows on TV. The bad news is that the information they trade upon is generally dismissed as being, well, *trivial*.

What we call "Trivia" are bits of information that are generally despised as irrelevant and unimportant in a society where the latter is a function of the former. As for the adjective "trivial"—it is as outright pejorative as "cheap" and "stupid"; the word cannot conceivably be honorific. Trivial is bad, and that's an end to it; although it's not always entirely that simple, given our temptation to dismiss information as trivial simply because somebody else knows it and we don't.

The irrelevance and unimportance that constitute triviality are, of course, highly negotiable. What is irrelevant and unimportant in one situation can be crucial in another; and since our lives are spent sorting through the mazes of different sorts of information, it follows that few things, if any, can be conclusively and absolutely judged as irrelevant and unimportant. The small details of our lives are so far from being trivial that to neglect or ignore them is nothing less than a human failure.

I can claim a certain authority in addressing this subject, because I have long collected old and rare books, an enterprise that most people seem to regard as just another hobby—a bit like collecting fruit jars, matchbook covers or those small paper vomit bags once carried in the seat pouches of commercial airplanes.[1] In the common view, to spend time and energy on bibliographical refinements of state, issue and edition, or in seeking out little-known ephemera of an obscure author or recondite subject, is an enterprise of desperate irrelevance and unimportance.

But even within this fribbling context, there are nuances and gradations of triviality. Collecting books on the presocratic philosophers or the American Civil War is likely to be judged less trivial than collecting the published memoirs of pop stars or 19th century books about Danish acrobats. And yet, even these straw figures might have the breath of life in them, because there is no intrinsic reason that a book about Danish acrobats (which, incidentally, I've never heard of) could not be more perceptive and perhaps even more profound than some ponderous treatise on the history of judicial systems or the moral decline of the West.

Among all the frivolous types of literature, there is one that is especially, immediately, recognizable as insignificant—books of anecdotes. Physicians are trained to be scornful of anecdotal evidence as unscientific; and in a literary context, anecdotes are conceded to be the most trivial form of narrative, standing at the opposite end of the spec-

---

[1] In his *The Birth of a Story* (Lon., 1972) William Sansom confesses to such a vice—obviously a more whimsical and idle affliction than the towering passions of the great Obsessives. And while it may seem that in my prefatory comments I have forfeited the right to stigmatize such deviant collectibles as trivial, I'll do it anyway and state that if there's any enterprise that can be so labelled, it's collecting the paper vomit bags from early jet aircraft. Even unused. And yet, even here, one should be cautious, for Sansom was no fool; he was a gifted writer, and if he had only taken the trouble to explain his motive for collecting these grotesque little disposables, it's just barely conceivable that he could have made it seem somehow intelligible.

trum from those massive novels whose great length alone qualifies them to be considered substantial, perhaps even significant. A book of anecdotes, however, promises nothing more than a brief and occasional amusement. They are books to "dip into," as we say, implying that they have no depths to put us in danger of drowning.

I am aware of this, and half agree with it, for it seems nothing less than common sense. A book of anecdotes is a nest of small birds, and serious readers are in search of bigger game. I understand this, but am not entirely convinced by it—partly because as an idle reader (the only untethered kind, after all) I can seldom gather the seriousness and discipline that large, monolithic tomes require for their full appreciation. Possessed of a trivial mind, I find books of anecdotes irresistible.

This was demonstrated, recently, when my wife and I signed up for a British Airways six-day tour, three days in London and three in Amsterdam. In London we saw a pair of clever one-act plays at the Comedy Theatre, and I visited my English literary agent in Clerkenwell; but I found our stay generally frustrating insofar as I was not able to spend enough time shopping for old books and departed without having bought a single volume—a rare occurrence, and a kind of failure.

The book acquisition had to wait for Amsterdam, where in the antiquarian section of DeSlegte's massive three-story bookstore, I came upon a volume titled *School-days of Eminent Men,* by John Timbs, bound in tan buckram and in very good original condition. First published in London, this edition was an American imprint, reprinted in Columbus, Ohio, in 1860. Listed at 75 guilders (nearly $40 in U.S. currency), it was overpriced; but I was intrigued by the simple fact of coming upon a copy of a book in Amsterdam which had first appeared in London, was then reprinted in Columbus, where I was born, and now awaited me in a foreign city I had never before visited.

As often happens when I hold a book in my hand, I found it mysterious and wonderful to contemplate its unique journey through time. By what tortuously unfathomable route of possession and exchange did it get *here,* wherever that might be? Such reflections are commonplace in the literature of bibliophily, and they often lead to silly gush, mystical vapours and cut-rate mysticism; nevertheless, at their heart, they are possessed of a truth as inescapable as time itself.

Furthermore, since *Schooldays* was nothing but a miscellany of anecdotes, the sort that appeals to trivial minds, I could not resist buying it. And I was not to be disappointed, for it is a repository of such riches, replete with curious stories and various arcane minutiae of life in olden times, that soon after I started reading it on our flight over the Atlantic, I knew that its having been printed in Columbus, Ohio, and my having chanced upon it in Amsterdam were compounded testimony that I was personally meant for this particular copy of this particular book, and it was meant for me.

To convey something of its abundance, I will begin where our lives begin, with women. Specifically, with the story of Dame Alice Owen, who started a free school in 1613, in memory of having been spared when a stray arrow flew through her cap, missing her head by only the breadth of her small finger.[2] As a teacher, I can think of no more fitting way to give thanks and celebrate one's survival of a close call than by founding a school. Unless it would be writing a book, which is, of course, a kind of school.

Timbs also retells the familiarly pathetic story of Lady Jane Grey, who died so young. On the morning of her execution, she tore a fly leaf from her Greek New Testament and wrote a letter in Greek to her sister; then in her notebook, she wrote three bravely self-exculpatory sentences in Greek, Latin and English. According to Thomas Fuller,

---

[2] While the great period of the bow and arrow as weaponry was past, archery was still vigorously pursued as a sport.

whom Timbs quotes: "She had the innocence of childhood, the beautie of youth, the solitude of middle, the gravitie of old age, and all at eighteen: the bust of a princesse, the learning of a clerk, the life of a saint, yet the death of a malefactor, for her parents' offences."

For today's reader, this doleful testimony is somewhat unsettled by the reference to Lady Jane Grey's bust, but the message remains sadly eloquent, nevertheless. It is followed by a livelier section titled "Sir Anthony Cook and His Four Learned Daughters." Like all 16th century girls of the nobility, they were instructed in Latin, Italian, French, an understanding of globes and astronomy, and how to play the lute. Sir Anthony's four daughters were all highly accomplished, but one of them, Anne, would be remembered especially, not only as an accomplished linguist and theologian, but as the mother of Francis Bacon.

Some of the anecdotes are as astonishing as they are amusing. Picture Oliver Cromwell as an infant being kidnapped from his cradle by a "great monkey" that carried him over the rooftops, while down below the family and neighbors gathered with blankets, hoping to catch him if he should be dropped. He was not dropped, of course; and history was fulfilled as we know it. (One likely reason he was not dropped is that the incident never happened; but mere fabrication should never ruin a good story.)

Living in the next century, Sir William Jones was a polyglot of astonishing attainment; even as a small boy, he showed such extraordinary gifts it was said of him that if he were left naked on Salisbury Plain, he could still find his way to fame and riches. Indeed, his entire life seemed to have been spent in relentless accomplishment. Not only did he become a great lawyer and Oriental scholar, but he excelled in all the European and classical languages, then went on to master Turkish, Arabic, Persian, Sanskrit, "Hindostanee and Bengalee," the omnivorous appetite of his massive intellect compelling him to assimilate a variety of more obscure Indian dialects. Unsatisfied with learning simply the rudiments, he mastered the literature of each country. And yet, when he died at the age of forty-seven, he remained frustrated by the fact that he had not yet *completely* mastered Chinese, Russian, Runic, Syrian, Ethiopic, Coptic, Dutch, Swedish and Welsh. Most of us in the Western world can understand something of his frustration, for we haven't mastered all of those languages, either.

It is not the anecdotes alone that enliven this lively book. Consider Thomas Fuller's method of composition, given in a footnote (where treasures can often be found, even in books with an indigent main text): in the first flush of creating, Fuller would write down the left side of a page the first word of each line as he envisioned it; then later, he would fill in the text. (I find this an utterly perplexing method, but that's how it is explained.) Or consider John Wesley, the founder of Methodism, who for fifty years arose at 4:00 am to study. He pursued learning so relentlessly, that he read even on horseback.

But it is the anecdotes that are best, after all. Consider the wonderful story about Arthur Wellesley, the Duke of Wellington, who left Eton with his brother to visit Lady Dungannon, a great gossip. The two boys decided to play a joke on their hostess by inventing some sort of outrageous lie, and decided to tell her that their sister, Anne, had just run off with the footman. When they saw how terribly shocked the old lady was, the two wags made her promise that she wouldn't tell a soul. Of course that's exactly what she did at her first opportunity, going to share the awful news with a neighbor. But when she returned, it was the boys who were astonished, for her neighbor already knew about it: their sister *had* run off with the footman.

Of all the anecdotes in John Timbs's book, I am most fond of what could be called Sir Walter Scott's "Parable of the Button." This little story alone was almost worth the price. According to virtually all that is known about him, Scott was not only a great novelist but something of a moral paragon.

He was amiable, honest, industrious, modest and charitable. And yet, he was human, of course; and Timbs tells of at least one instance in which he proved capable of low cunning.

As a small boy, Scott was constantly frustrated by a schoolmate who always stood at the top of the class. Brilliant as he himself was, and knew himself to be, Scott could not overtake this prodigy, who in his recitals inevitably proved to have mastered his lessons to utter perfection. Then one day Scott noticed that when he answered the schoolmaster's questions, this lad always fumbled with his fingers at a particular button on his waistcoat.

Scott's notice of such a fact, and his inference therefrom, are manifestations of genius; and "in an evil moment" he decided that when the boy hung his coat up, he would take his knife and cut the button off. The rest should be told in Scott's own words, as reported by Timbs: "Great was my anxiety to know the success of my measure; it succeeded too well. When the boy was again questioned, his fingers sought again for the button, but it was not to be found. In his distress he looked down for it; it was to be seen no more than to be felt. He stood confounded, and I took possession of his place; nor did he ever recover it, or ever, I believe, suspect who was the author of his wrong. . . . "

Beginning writers are often cautioned against using the passive voice, and like most counsel available for teaching the subject, this is not without merit. Even so, the crisis in this Parable of the Button is conveyed by so memorable a use of the passive voice that it could not be improved upon: "When the boy was again questioned, his fingers sought again for the button, but it was not to be found." The simple eloquence of that statement is as grand as it is elusive to final analysis.[3]

---

[3] This reference to what might be called the "symbol of the missing button" brings to mind a story, not in Timbs' book, about Kant, who, while lecturing, was so distracted by the sight of a missing button on a student's coat that he lost his train of thought.

———

Who was the author who had brought all these morsels of anecdote together? I had never heard of John Timbs, and was naturally curious; so, like Timbs himself, I began to gather bits and pieces from various sources to arrive at some sense of who he was and what he was like. It turns out that there is very little information about him, but enough to say that he was born in 1801 and by the time he died in 1875, had published over 150 volumes—one of that great sad majority of writers whose momentary fame is destined to be swallowed by oblivion. And like a majority within that sad majority, after all his seeming success in publishing so many books, Timbs died in poverty.

However, I did come upon one fact that immediately stood out: Timbs was born in Clerkenwell, the very location of my literary agent whose office I had visited in London only three days before. Here was still another mystical connection for those of us who like to contemplate the workings of chance and often pause to marvel over the intricate dance of coincidence.

Timbs, himself, would have understood this, for he was addicted to curiosities as he was to anecdotes, two appetites with much in common. The titles of his books bear witness to his enthusiasm for the marvelous and his penchant for contemplating odd connections: *Nooks and Corners of English Life, Signs Before Death, Things Not Generally Known, Wine-Drinker's Manual, Illustrated Book of Wonders, Historic Ninepins: A Book of Curiosities, Curiosities of London, A Century of Anecdotes, 1760 to 1860,* and on and on.

You can see from the above list of titles that some of his books were written for the young, a still-growing readership in the 19th century, the age of the Common Reader. But his success was not limited to any particular audience. "Mr. Timbs possesses the rare faculty of clear and accurate condensation," the *London Lancet* proclaimed; and *The London Athenaeum* announced that "Any one who reads and remembers Mr. Timbs's encyclopaedic varieties should ever after be a good tea-table talker, an excellent companion for children, a 'well-read person,' and a proficient lecturer."

It is obvious, however, that his gift for the marvelous is not limited to tea-table talk and the sensibilities of children. His literary preoccupations with anecdotes and the celebration of small things show that Timbs had the faculty of wonder, a flair for seeing behind the dull familiarity of things that mirrors our own dullness. And his vitality and enthusiasm are everywhere infectious. In commenting upon his *Romance of London,* the *London Saturday Review* wrote: "We doubt whether a more entertaining compilation has ever been made for the delectation of Londoners."

Such delectation is not limited to Londoners, of course; it extends to Amsterdam and Columbus, Ohio and passengers on transatlantic flights . . . and no doubt to many other places where copies of his books have drifted in their intricate patterns of ownership and exchange throughout the years, being available for people, even today, to pick up and read some of the latest news from another place and another time, written by one who is almost—but for that reason alone, not quite—forgotten.

2

The Binding of Books and the Matter of Spirit

*O*ne day in the late 1890s, the young Winston Churchill visited an office of the Conservative Party to inquire about a possible career in politics. When he was informed by the official that if he didn't raise a significant sum of money, his opportunities would be seriously diminished, Churchill was discouraged (or at least as discouraged as it is possible to imagine him). But when he was about to leave the office, he saw something that would change his life. Years later, he would describe this seemingly small event as follows:

> My eye lighted upon a large book on his table on the cover of which was a white label bearing the inscription 'SPEAKERS WANTED.' I gazed upon this with wonder. Fancy that! Speakers were wanted and here was a bulky book of applications! Now I had always wanted to make a speech; but I had never on any occasion great or small been invited or indeed allowed to do so.[1]

This was a magic moment for the young Winston, an opening into a future giddy with promise, excitement and adventure. For him, the label bearing the words *Speakers Wanted* had the evocative power of that sign Alice encountered in Wonderland. Like "Drink me," "Speakers Wanted" hinted

---

[1] *A Roving Commission,* NY, 1941, p.204.

at both an eventuation and transformation suggestive of some mysterious though triumphant future—a future, one might fancy in retrospect, waiting to be found inside the book's covers.

Our custom of gift-wrapping presents reflects such a notion, and is therefore, and in its way, mysterious. You can bring a naked bottle of wine to a dinner party or simply hand over an unwrapped book as a birthday gift without risking too great an impropriety; and yet, the gesture leaves us with a sense of compromise and incompleteness. Part of a gift is missing if it is not wrapped, and that something is ceremonial and symbolic. An unwrapped present is somewhat like an unbound book, or perhaps one that *is* bound, but lacks a label—a label, perhaps, with the words, *Speakers Wanted*.

Ceremonies and symbols are in themselves mysterious because they are instruments of distance, meant for probing realities otherwise unknowable. No matter how attractive and desirable it may otherwise be, an unwrapped gift is incomplete, for it lacks momentary promise. Breaking into a box knowing that it contains something unknown is essential to the ceremony. The gift you have received exists in time, *in* the present, and whatever use or desirability it will have for you as a future possession will be forever threaded through that brief moment of anticipation when you were forced to open the package in order to discover its inner truth.

Though evanescent, this moment of expectation is real and inescapable. In spite of his glorious career as an orator, Churchill could never have quite recaptured the *specific* thrill of promise implicit in that first instant of discovery. No matter how fine or expensive or touchingly personal the gift within, it cannot in the nature of things be possessed of the same charm as the moment of its anticipation. "Heard melodies are sweet, but those unheard are sweeter." And so it is with gifts, some of whose promissory grace inevitably vanishes in the light of actuality.

By now, we have come a long way from the common-sense view that mysteries are confined to those unseen presences concealed by the packages that contain them. Exteriors also have their own mysteries, as well—even though these are by definition, and at first glimpse, visible. And along with their containing innerness, they partake of their own uniquenesses, as if there were another spatial dimension that cannot be measured. In addition to signifying depth, surfaces have their own sort of depth—let us say, lateral rather than vertical.

But what is a *lateral* depth? How can depth be measured sideways and forward rather than down? In this sense, would two acres of land be twice as deep as one? What sort of nonsense is that? And yet, surfaces are never more than partially visible, which means that when we focus upon this part, the remainder is as surely lost to sight as the dreamlike interior of the eeriest grotto. Its retrievability is no more than a promise, like that of the secret gift within a package. So in this sense, two acres really *are* twice as deep as one.

Obsessed with the inscrutable depth of a canvas surface, painters understand such a truth instinctively.

———————

Now, the long loop of my preamble brings us naturally back to the subject of book bindings, whose ostensible object is to package and protect the leaves of a text. Since they provide a tempting surface for decoration, that temptation has naturally proved irresistible. Over a millennium after those first bindings were designed to embrace and preserve the leaves of a book, the first dust jackets—covers conceived to cover the covers—passed through the same phased development of austere plainness to decorative excess, somewhat in the manner of all new inventions, imitating that original evolutionary invention of ontogeny recapitulating phylogeny. Translations everywhere.

As for bindings, the temptation they provide for embellishment was felt so early in their history that by the fifth century A.D., St. Jerome cried out to the wealthy collectors of his day: "Your books are covered with precious stones, and Christ dies naked before the door of his temple!" Jerome's cry has been muted by the centuries, and its echoes are no longer haunted by so dour a theology, but the sentiment lives on. Essentially, its premise is that books are instruments, therefore means to an end; and to convert means into ends and lavish excessive care upon them is not only foolish, it is wrong. And to the extent that decadence can be defined as a loss of the object, *decadent.*

Most of us draw a line between wholesomeness and decadence, but we draw it differently, and in different places. (We also lean toward a different terminology, for in a decadent age, the word "wholesome" is a cultural embarrassment.) Seventeenth-century American books were an almost exclusively New England products, therefore bound puritanically in plain leather—the gold-tooled binding of Increase Mather's 1679 *A Call From Heaven* an exception. At the other end of the spectrum are the Kelmscott productions of William Morris, whose pages and bindings are cicatrized with as baroque an excess of design as has ever embellished or mutilated a surface.

But it is an anecdote about Morris's disciple, T. J. Cobden-Sanderson, that conveys the right proportion. When a lady bibliophile complained to him that the six pounds he'd charged for a binding with very little gold tooling seemed exorbitant, he is said to have answered: "Madam, I charge as much for my restraint as for my elaboration."

Tacitus' *De Vita Et Moribus Julii Agricolae* was the first book printed by the Doves Press, and it was designed by Cobden-Sanderson. Bound in plain vellum, the book is an almost unbearably exquisite expression of the restraint he spoke of. It is also a just example of the high standard of excellence generally maintained by the Doves Press, whose productions were characterized, in the words of Douglas C.

McMurtrie, "by a majestic simplicity of design, meticulous type-setting, flawless presswork on the finest of papers and workmanlike binding." The result, as manifest in this edition of Tacitus, is perhaps too austere for some tastes, but not for mine. And yet, can it be said to be designed at all, if it is virtually plain? (I'm afraid that will take some thought, and I'd rather not.)

Cobden-Sanderson's range of accomplishment was broad, and some of his bindings, like that of Swinburne's *Atalanta In Calydon*, are splendidly ornate, risking excess ornament very much as his Doves Press bindings tend to risk too little. Many of his contemporaries liked to refer to Cobden-Sanderson's "genius"; and the term is perhaps justified when one considers his philosophical grasp of, not just bookmaking, as it is narrowly considered, but the symbolic role of the book as both cultural instrument and aesthetic object.

"The ideal book," he wrote in his book of that title, "is a composite thing, made up of many parts, and may be made beautiful by the beauty of each of its parts . . . in subordination to the whole which collectively they constitute . . . On the other hand each contributory part may usurp the functions of the rest and of the whole, and growing beautiful beyond all bounds ruin for its own the common cause."

Such wisdom is hardly limited to books; it applies to the components of all art as well as to the collaborative human effort required by such diverse entities as baseball teams, committees, and corporations—not to mention democracy itself. Like so many of our values, the grace of that internal harmony and elegant concinnity praised by Cobden-Sanderson is felt most acutely in its absence and neglect. Individuals who sacrifice the common good for their own personal aggrandizement are like those "parts" the great bookman spoke of—a lavish binding wasted upon pulp leaves, for example; or a thick rag paper marred by cheap and clumsy typesetting, utilizing a crudely designed font.

The sacrifice of a public good for personal glorification is always painful, whether in the hot-dog behavior of a sports star or the finagling of an ambitious politico . . . bringing to mind those fractious lines of Dryden, which seem especially pertinent to the gang-warfare of contemporary politics (you may of course supply the names of your own representatives here, as at the voting booth):

> "In friendship false, implacable in hate,
> Resolved to ruin or to rule the state."

———

It is a paradox that when we speak of a book's "matter," we are speaking of that which is not matter at all, but *noumenon*, *gestalt*, transcendent form, idea—that which is implicit in, and conveyed by, the sequence of the words in the text. Thus it is precisely the "matter" of Isaac Walton's *The Compleat Angler* that remains unaltered behind all its changing materials, with their variations of print, paper and binding in the more than 300 editions of its publishing history. The matter is the order of the words, not their material representations in print. As those literate barbarians who don't collect books like to proclaim: it's the *matter* that matters, not the edition.

This matter they speak of is the book's "mind," not its physical mass. It is the essence, the soul, the ghost, in the book's body. It is the secret, inner life, which we know exists but don't know exactly *how* it exists, or what it is, or— as I am finding out at this very moment—how, precisely, to describe it. This inner life of the book is very much like our own inner life, which is the ultimate mystery of innerness. We know this about ourselves, and yet keep trying to ignore it in the name of clarity and scientific integrity.

Still, scholars in the humanities love a mystery; that is why so many of them read and collect mystective novels. It is axiomatic for them that, in spite of their exasperating inaccessibility to formulation, mysteries are intrinsic to whatever is meant by "reality." It is precisely in their combining the immeasurably enigmatic and the inescapably authentic that certain questions fascinate and beguile the mind. And yet, if they were entirely mysterious and beyond measure, how could anything at all be known about them?

There is only one way—through their outer dress, their envelopes, their bodies. We assume a vital though mysterious connection between inner and outer realities, and indeed have no other way of knowing them, for they are transactionals, each requiring the other for its status as validity or truth. In this way, and to this extent, we know books by their bindings; if we didn't, whenever we opened a book we would have no idea what text would be waiting to surprise us.

What if it were otherwise? What if all the books in a library had their bindings removed and were then recased at random, so that *Gone With The Wind* would be found in the binding for a Second Year Algebra text, and Nabokov's *Pnin* would be bound in the *1941 Blue Jacket's Manual*? Then, truly, you could not judge a book by its cover. But until such mad transformations occur, and within obvious limitations, we can assume otherwise.

Looked at closely, the outer coverings of things always partake of their plenary significance. In one of his journals, the prudish Hawthorne observed that clothing has become as natural for us as our bodies, and an essential part of our human nature. That this is still true is perversely implicit in the popularity of such magazines as *Playboy* and *Penthouse*. Without clothing, we are as incomplete as an unbound book. Many years ago, a wealthy collector had all of his acquisitions handsomely rebound, saying that he liked his friends to be well-dressed.

Exteriors, being phenomenal, are not only essential to the world of things as we know them, they are intrinsically mysterious. In saying that containers "contain" mysteries, we usually mean that they enclose that which is entirely separate, and both literally and figuratively hidden. And yet, those surfaces are cryptic in themselves, quite apart from what they conceal and protect. Thus, the binding of a book is the outer, physical form of three sorts of mystery: the visible text, that text's invisible "meaning," and the binding itself as a physical entity.

And yet, the tension between inner and outer meanings is not limited to this primary, spatial mode; it applies to the basic structure of the metaphor, in which the vehicle, or literal meaning, is external, and the tenor, or intended meaning, is figurative and interior. In this, it is like the matter of a book, when that matter refers to its "message" or "meaning." Much of the point and effort of literary study is focused upon the exegesis of latent, textual meanings . . . mining texts for occult implications and the bright gold of allusion.

In past centuries allegorical and metaphorical ways of thinking were of great, even obsessive, interest, occasionally extending upwards into heights of pure madness, especially in the rarified atmosphere of religious controversy, where there is little oxygen. With the advancement of science, Biblical interpretations became increasingly metaphorical in their forced retreat from literal meaning, so that the 969 years Methuselah was said to have lived turned out to be not years after all, but some lesser interval of time.

The belief that overt facts conceal mysterious essences was an old one, and it found its way into strange places. The ancient story of Jason and the Golden Fleece was especially hospitable to allegorical interpretation. Scholars since antiquity occupied themselves with the Euhemeristic passion to seek out some kind of historical, factual basis for the events celebrated in *The Argonautica.*

This habitude, combined with a passion for parables, inspired some extraordinary interpretations. There were those who equated the golden fleece with rain and fertility.

Others interpreted the Argonauts' quest as a solar myth, the ram being associated with Zeus, whose image was the sun. Furthermore, the Argonauts voyaged into the unknown East to bring back a golden (i.e., shining) object. To others, the Golden Fleece was a symbol of human purity. In still another view, the ram was a variation upon the Lamb of God, or Christ.

Last but not least, and most germane to our present purpose, was a theory advanced by an obscure tenth century scholar named Suidas, that the golden fleece was not simply the resplendent hide of a great ram, but the sheepskin binding of a book on alchemy. The form of this intriguing notion exemplifies its purport. As the cover of a book both conceals and represents its text and the matter therein, so does the literal meaning of the Golden Fleece function figuratively, concealing and representing the arcane formula for the transmutation of metals into higher forms.

Who was this Suidas who propounded such an astonishing interpretation, one that retrojects alchemical lore into a far more distant past than can be documented elsewhere? I have found little information about him; he is known chiefly for his *Suda Lexicon*—evidently not much of a lexicon at all, in the modern sense of the word, but a sort of notional encyclopaedia filled with folklore, superstitions and various whimsical conceits, including the above-mentioned theory.

So far as I can tell, the *Suda Lexicon* has never been translated from its original Greek into English. After considerable effort, I was able to procure a copy through the inter-library loan system of the university where I teach. Immediately upon opening the book, however, I saw that the Greek was a briarpatch, with only the most exiguous notes in German and Latin—in themselves of limited usefulness to me—although I can sometimes make out the sense of a passage in the intersection of my smattering of all three languages.

But here there was no help, so I walked around the briarpatch, telling myself that it was something I could probably translate if my life depended upon it; then immediately comforting myself with the realization that my life *didn't* depend upon it. So I returned the book forthwith and lapsed into the serene repose of my previously undisturbed ignorance.

You pay a price for everything, of course; and the price I am paying for my laziness is an unscratchable itch. What *were* Suidas' reasons for thinking that the Golden Fleece was actually the binding of a book about transmuting baser elements into gold? What could they have been? On the surface (in a manner of speaking), the idea seems absurd. In the *Argonautica* of Apollonius of Rhodes, the text that conveys the fullest version of the story, the sheepskin is said to be large enough to hang over Jason's shoulder and reach the ground. A *ram* that size? More like an elephant folio.

But, of course, not even a mythical ram could be truly elephantine; and that wasn't the sort of book referred to, anyway. The reference would have been to a papyrus roll, and its "binding" would have been a sort of leather pouch, called a *diphthera*. Suidas evidently believed that the leather was parchment, or sheepskin; and that the text contained the long-sought alchemist's formula.

Since the fleece was said to be golden, transmutation was probably the book's primary focus, although arriving at a formula for transmuting baser metals into gold was only part of the alchemists' quest. According to Paracelsus, the "Double Tincture" had to do with curing diseases as well as transmuting metals into a higher form—gold being the highest. As for Suidas himself: the tenth century in which he lived was a time when the influx of Arabic learning into Europe was very great, and much of that learning was in the form of astrological and alchemical lore—the word *alchemy* itself being from the Arabic, meaning "the art of transformation," and by a tortuous historical linguistic route the origin of our word "chemistry."

Recently I bought a very obscure alchemical treatise—a 16mo bound in quarter leather and marbled boards, with gilt title on red leather. The title page is in itself an abstract of the book (as is typical of the period), and reads as follows:

THE
GOLDEN ASS
WELL MANAGED
AND
MYDAS Restored to Reason

Or a new Chymical Light appearing as a day Star of
Comfort to all under Oppression or Calamities, as well
Illiterate, as Learned, Male as Female; to ease their
Burdens and provide for their Families.

WHEREIN
The Golden Fleece is Demonstrated to the blind world, and
that good Gold may be found as well in Cold as Hot
Regions (though better in hot) within and without through
the universal Globe of the Earth, and be profitably
extracted: So that in all places where any Sand, Stones,
Gravel, or Flints are, you cannot so much as place your
footing, but you may find both Gold, and the true matter of
the Philosopher's Stone. And is a Work of Women and
play of Children.

Written at Amsterdam, 1669. by *John Rodolf Glauber*, The
bright Sun of our Age, and Lover of Mankind, like a true
Elias riding on this Golden Ass, in a Fiery Chariot.

———

And Translated out of Latin into English, in briefer Notes,
1670 by *W. C* . Esq. True Lover of Art and Nature, and well
wisher to all men, especially to the poor distressed
Houshold of Faith; The true Catholick Church, and body of
Christ, Dispersed through many Forms of Religions,
through the whole World, as the perfect *Israelites*.

Note here a typical seventeenth-century version of a dust-jacket puff, touched with the philo-semitism of the time, and praising the author and translator as virtual saints. Indeed, we are meant to understand that these were two benevolent men—and whoever might possess their book and apply its nostrums for transmuting sand and gravel and such into gold is blessed. Literally construed, that blessing might have a greater authority than first appears, and touch upon the supernatural, for Glauber died in 1668—in which case, if the biographical note of *The Golden Ass, Well-Managed* is to be believed, he wrote it in Amsterdam a year after he'd died.

The title's reference is of course to the old story of King Midas, who was asked to judge a musical contest, and declared Pan the winner over Apollo. Insulted, Apollo changed his ears into those of an ass—the dream of many a poet when stung by a bad review. Later, of course, Midas was granted his wish that all he touched would turn to gold—a classic moral showing how little we know what's good for us. But, as the title page announces, through Glauber's "new Chymical Light," Midas has finally been restored to reason.

Glauber has a modest place in the history of science. A contemporary of Newton, he was one of those transitional figures—half alchemist, half-chemist—who participated in standing old notions on their heads, thus making way for the scientific revolution. He was said to have developed an early method for manufacturing acids and salts, but was considered a charlatan because of his secret concoction, *Sal Mirabile,* a cathartic. Open channels of communication are the lifeblood of science, but death to humbugs.

One of the interesting features of *The Golden Ass* is that many of the prescriptions for transmuting baser metals into gold are not about transmutation at all; they are about the *discovery* of gold in various ores and its refinement therefrom. In spite of his liberal references to Paracelsus, Glauber is as intent upon showing how gold is identified and extracted as upon how it is manufactured from humbler stones and ores. In many passages an innocent reader can't be sure which process is being described: transmutation or discovery. And, indeed, Glauber's uncertain poise between these quite different processes reflects his transitional character as half-alchemist and half-chemist.

This ambiguity, however, is not all there is; it is compounded with a spiritual one. Glauber tells us so. "But now," he writes, "the philosophers seek not corporeal gold, but spiritual." And here, finally, another loop is closed, and we return to the basic theme of a material envelope covering a spiritual truth. So it is that the vehicle, or literal meaning, of a metaphor carries its tenor, or figurative meaning; and a reference to golden fleece conceals a formula for transcending nature; and the material binding of a book conceals its inner physical matter in the form of printed pages . . . which in turn contain its intellectual or spiritual matter, what we mean when we say we have read the same book in different editions.

———————

One of the most interesting and eloquent statements upon the aesthetics of book bindings can be found in the ninth edition (one of the two "scholars' editions") of *The Encyclopaedia Brittanica*, as follows:

At the time when books were rarities, being either manuscripts produced by patient secluded labour or the productions of the printing-press during the infancy of typography, they were naturally very highly prized; and as much labour and expense were bestowed upon the protection and embellishment of a cherished folio as would suffice at the present day for the building of a house. The wooden cover of a book, with its metal hinges, bosses, guards, and clasps, seems, in all but dimensions, fit for a church door.

Like all those examples previously given, houses and church doors are containers of mystery, and worthy of our respect in themselves, for the profound depths of their surfaces as well as for those more obvious depths they conceal and contain. And there is one perspective in which it is as just and comprehensible for bibliophiles to rejoice in the care lavished upon the exteriors of their possessions as it is for others to take pleasure in a finely made house or the elegantly carved door of a church.

We can't read all our books all the time, but daily we can contemplate their spines lining the shelves of our libraries. These are what collectors look at, and they look at them differently, according to their individual aesthetics, needs and temperaments. Some look upon them as big-game hunters look upon their trophies—both sorts of trophies, in the case of older books, displaying the tanned and treated hides of animals; others look upon their books as mirrors of what they are or would like to be.

These collectors are sentimentalists, of course; but what would life be without sentiment—even the sort that extends to that extremity stigmatized as "sentimentality"? Too many wise and accomplished people have had their years enriched by such possessions, along with the memory of how they were acquired, for anyone to dismiss their passions as trivial or irrelevant.

All true. And yet, in closing, it must be pointed out that surfaces without interiors are nothing but a mockery. It is ultimately the magic within that justifies the magic without. It is the printed text that validates the beautiful workmanship of bindings and renders it meaningful. Whatever is alive is admirable and mysterious, and however life is defined, it is interior—it exists somewhere inside—a truth that all surfaces proclaim, celebrate, and serve.

Samuel Taylor Coleridge understood this, but in understanding it, lost his balance and went too far, falling into a Coleridgean fit. In 1802 he told his wife: "I love warm rooms, comfortable fires, & food, books, natural scenery, music &c." So far, you will say, so good. But then the great man's good sense tilted and he staggered into incoherence, saying: ". . . but I do not care what *binding* the Books have, whether they are dusty or clean—& I *dislike* . . . all the ordinary symbols & appendages of artificial superiority—or what is called *Gentility*."

It's a pity he could not have achieved a sensible balance between inner and outer validities, so obviously legitimate in themselves and so easily reconciled. It's a pity he had to set these values at each other's throat, like pit bulls or fighting cocks, rather than working their contrarieties together to achieve a dialectic fusion and synthesis. Interiors and exteriors are transactionals, after all; and it is fitting that they should be joined. Since books are designed to be read, it is only reasonable that some of us should take care that the eye is pleased.

Even so the principle bears repetition: to lavish care upon the bindings of books with an utter and total disregard of their content is not only an intellectual sin, it is foolishness. There have been a few such pathetic members in the long and honorable tradition of bibliophily, and they are as deserving of our pity as of Robert Burns' satiric scorn in his little poem, "The Bookworms":

> Through and through the inspiréd leaves,
> Ye maggots, make your windings;
> But, oh!, respect his lordship's tastes,
> And spare his golden bindings!

And that golden feminine rhyme may serve as the back cover of my little essay, fitting to close it with a thud...along with my own brief expression of personal thanks that, while this small and pleasant quatrain was written by Robert Burns, it was not done in the Scottish dialect.

3

Words from the Smokehouse: The Vituperations of Theophilus Noel

*I*t's obvious that anybody who sits down to write a book has to be a little unbalanced. Who has the authority to stake a claim upon the attention of strangers? By what mandate does a writer presume to command your notice? The cause is egotism, of course; and egotism is madness. And yet, it is not entirely unnatural, because what we are is all we have to be, the only vessels at our disposal for containing the world; our selves are our sole instruments for mirroring the universe and making sense out of it. How could such an arrangement ever conceivably be devoid of egotism?

So maybe it's no wonder that in succumbing to the pressure of our feelings and prejudices, we become obsessed, and seek some sort of relief by unloading them— first into the commodious tolerance of language, and then upon the public. The tension builds and builds until we suddenly find ourselves at the keyboard, contriving sentences. This is all true; but it's still egotism, and its traces can be found everywhere. Even here, on this growing page, as I write. And, now, as you read.

Such lunacy is intensified and compounded, however, when writers pay to have their infatuations printed. Submitting to a vanity press, or self-publishing on one's own, is generally an evasion and a fraud. Paying to have a book published does not make people *writers* any more than putting on a uniform would make them soldiers. And even though self-publishing is only slightly more egomaniacal than doing it the conventional way, paying for the manufacture of your own book is peculiarly desperate and pathetic.

Even so, there is a very small class of self-publishers who are worthy of remembrance though forgotten. Or *almost* forgotten—as is the case with my present subject, Theophilus Noel, whose *Autobiography and Reminiscences* was published in 1904, in Chicago, by—what else?—the "Theo. Noel Printing Company." It's doubtful that this company ever published another book; but no matter, for this one title justifies its existence, having more life in its twelve-word Preface than the entire contents of some books brought out by real publishers.

Indeed, it was the preface which caught my attention years ago in an antiquarian bookshop when I picked up a quarto bound in tough maroon cloth, with gilt lettering on front and spine. I opened it and came upon the the following words engraved in the holograph scrawl of the author: "Preface. If you don't like my Bacon, don't come to my Smokehouse again. Yours truly, Theophilus Noel."

Then, when I turned to the opening of the chapter titled "Boyhood Days," I knew this was a book I had to buy.

> It was in the middle of the year when the campaign cry was hard cider and log cabins that I was born, and for why I ofttimes think I love apples and all other sorts of fruits that will make as many good things as they do. I was born in a log cabin on a puncheon floor, and was rocked in a sap trough. That log cabin has long since passed away, but not my remembrance of it and of its environments, the tall trees of the southwestern part of the Wolferine State.

The quaint eccentricity of the phrasing—especially "for why I ofttimes think"—and the general awkwardness throughout might have been enough to discourage the editor of a real publisher, supposing Noel had submitted his manuscript to one; but for a reader with the leisure to savor the language, this small sample already reveals a prose that is tough, vivid, insightful and just a little bit cussed. Like its creator, this writing might have been born on a puncheon floor and rocked in a sap trough.

The promise in these grand openings is not betrayed anywhere in the 340 pages that follow. Heraclitus claimed that war is the father of all things, and Noel was at war with practically everything in sight, and a number of things that weren't. He was singularly and uncommonly gifted in disapproval, intolerance, bull-headedness, bigotry and wrath, and the stories he tells about his experiences in the Civil War and the old west are as lively and fascinating as any I have ever seen brought out by a respectable publisher.

In short, Theophilus Noel was an extraordinary human being, and his autobiography is an extraordinary document. Like the most interesting eccentrics, Noel tended to be just as clear-headed as he was wrong-headed, and often managed to do both at the same time. It's no wonder that a man with such cranky, tough-minded gifts was forced to write about his life and opinions, then self-publish the result.

———————

It is interesting to contemplate the notion that the mystery of a writer's style is everywhere manifest in a text. But is this true? Dickens and Eliot and Trollope could all write sentences and even whole passages that are dull and silly, so that if theoretically naive readers were to dip into one of their books, their sampling might not be at all representative of the author's great gifts. Even writers with a more homogeneous style, like Hemingway, can betray themselves in small portions, so that their excellences can be missed by chance acquaintance.

Nevertheless, in one way or another, we reveal ourselves constantly, in everything we do; every act, no matter how inconsequential in a practical sense, conveys something of what we are. Our personal testimony is inevitable and relentless, and there's nothing we can do or say to conceal it. "Do not *say* things," Emerson wrote in his August 9, 1840, Journal entry. "What you *are* stands over you the while and thunders so that I cannot hear what you say to the contrary." And even though Emerson may be said to have *said* it, this is as true as the akimbo elbows of paradox.

There is certainly no concealing the fire that snaps, crackles and blazes in the hearth of this cantankerous rascal, Theophilus Noel. After recounting how as a boy he'd been cheated by purchasing a pocket knife for forty-two cents (paid with twenty-one "two cent pieces"), he noted with satisfaction that the fellow who'd cheated him "died in the poorhouse." Then, sounding perversely and defiantly self-righteous, Noel says, "I never treated boy, man, nigger or Indian that way, which accounts for the large number of I O U's there are out over the country in my favor, and always will be."

The word "nigger" is, of course, offensive; and today, in virtually all contexts, it is judged *taboo*; but to pretend that the *word* does not exist is both silly and dishonest, and to refer to it indirectly as the "n word"—in line with recent usage at the O.J. Simpson trial—is utterly and inexcusably vapid. Forbidding it implies that the word is a vessel filled with such poisonous matter that it should not be opened and aired. But if, beyond the purviews of superstition and ignorance, such a metaphor had any validity whatsoever, it would be better to air those contents than to keep them sealed up, festering with the virulence of racist hatred and fostering the politically correct hypocrisies of our time.

The vocabulary of the quoted passage is typical, as are the sentiments behind it. Noel will find occasions in the book to recite all the cant of bigotry, seldom failing to add a few flourishes of his own. In one place, he says that it is part of the African's nature to be "indolent, insolent and thievish." In another, he likens them to cats, who "have little or no thoughts of the past and no gratitude in their makeup." It does not seem to occur to him that whatever truth can be found in such generalizations might have something to do with the institution of slavery; and when he refers to these African slaves as "the devils that brought [disaster] upon the South," his confusion of cause and effect has a certain grandiose irresponsibility about it.

Blacks are not the exclusive target of Noel's bigotry, but they are the most obvious and most frequently mentioned. In referring to the contemporary distribution of wealth in the South, he predictably says that it is largely owned by "Jews and foreign corporations." And yet, his very dislikes and intolerance are possessed of a large and perverse sort of tolerance, in the sense that there is no group or class or race that is exempt from his detestation. His disapproval of virtually every group identity saps his disapproval of invidiousness. He fires his volleys in all directions. Union soldiers and the Federal government are found despicable, of course; but so are the Rebel soldiers, his own comrades, whose lies about the cruelties they'd experienced in Union prisons he found especially disgusting and offensive.

No class of people escapes his censure—not even newspaper readers. In Noel's view, these poor, helpless, ignorant wretches submit to having their opinions molded by editorial spin. "I have no more of a respectable [*sic*] opinion of such men in these United States than I have for a low-down, depraved, ignorant, vicious Mexican bull, cock and dog fighter." The incoherence of this sentence is almost worthy of our admiration. It can be said to have more heat than light, but not more smoke than fire, because it burns murkily, ending with a creature possessed of an impenetrable mystery. Or is that *creatures*? Whichever it is, or might be, how did *Mexico* get sucked down the mighty drain of his abhorrence? Possibly for no other reason than its sounding good or just being an available notion.

But the sad and happy truth is, there was no limit to the objects of this man's disgust. He called most things as he saw them, and to see them was to see red . . . as in his remembering the Red River, when he was with the Texas cavalry: "The Federal gunboats came down the river, one right close behind the other, the first four in advance loaded down with cripples, convalescents and sick, and the mail. It was a beautiful sight to see those boats coming round the bend, decked with the flags of *our nation* and well banded with good players and blowers and horn tooters. If ever there was any one thing I did hate worse than another it was two toot-horns worse than one."

Indeed, if there was any one thing this choleric man hated worse than another it was *any* two things, and to hell with them, whatever in the hell they were.

———————

For all its bombast and fury, the vocabulary of Noel's autobiography was obviously tamed to accommodate the politeness required by the Edwardian sensibilities of his time. In 1904 he would have had trouble finding a printer to set up a text with such words as "bastard" or "son of a bitch" in it, let alone the raunchy diction of our more enlightened age. And yet, even though it is free of profanity and obscenity, you have to believe that the man who wrote this book was a first-class cusser, a maledictor of great attainment, a Pap Finn afflicted with, and complicated by, a certain degree of intelligence and personal hygiene. After reading the first dozen pages, it is impossible to believe that in his private life Theophilus Noel was anything less than an artist of scabrousness and execration.

Late in the book, he comes right out and tells us so, employing that venerable figure of speech known as litotes: "It has not been seldom in my day that I have been compelled to paint the air so blue a buzzard could not fly in it,

and fill it with fumes that a saint could not live in, in order
to get rid of devils and bring about a harmonious and profitable adjustment of affairs."

This passage bears testimony to the fact that Noel's
mind was a curious blend of vividness and chaos. Throughout his book, one finds perfect lucidity alternating with wild
and sometimes perplexing divagations. Even so, the little
anecdotes and parables are some of the best parts, and most
of them are admirably composed, within their brief scope,
even when one does not entirely approve of the sentiments
they embody.

Indeed, it is conceivable that a natural gift for story
telling and political responsibility are incompatible, since
the one despises sobriety and the other requires it. Perhaps.
But whatever the validity of this generalization (and it is
problematical, to be sure—as any profane and foul-
mouthed politician can swear to), these attributes are evident discrepancies in the character of Theophilus Noel. He
seems to know it, but remains defiant in his eccentricities,
and proud of his ability to snare the interest of readers,
regardless of their sensitivity and allegiance. "If you have
read this far," he brags on the twenty-eighth page, "you will
read further."

Which is true, because of the colorful expressiveness
of his language and his wonderful yarns—many of which,
like many of the best stories, have to do with human superstition and folly. In one, he tells of a preacher who was
asked to pray for rain, which the parson accomplished with
such alarming success that he was then asked to pray for it
to stop. This reads like the sort of folk yarn Mark Twain
might have picked up and dusted off for his repertoire on
the speaking circuit; but I like to think it was something
Theophilus Noel witnessed, or heard about, or made up,
and then stored in his memory.

Then there's the story about the great divining rod
scam, an instrument which after Reconstruction was de-

vised by a "cunning, slick, plausible, two-faced, stem-winding Yankee." According to Noel, after the Civil War, almost all southerners, black or white, were obsessed with reports and legends about vast hordes of gold and silver coins and diamond jewelry buried somewhere on their land. Given this popular delusion, it was perhaps only natural that some "cunning, slick, plausible" Yankee villain should arrive to promote his scheme with vigor throughout the South:

> His advertisement was short, pointed and sweet and in substance said that he was the inventor, discoverer, owner, and absolue possessor of a divining rod, a magnetized-electro-poised-ozone-fluted-pole-twisting-guaranteed-to-find-buried-silver and gold, jewels, etc., secreted by anybody, anywhere. Particulars furnished upon application.

All of this sounds pretty impressive—especially, when you consider that this was long before the invention and availability of modern metal-detectors. Since the divining rod was, of course, utterly worthless, the Yankee villain got wealthy, while those poor infatuated canoodles he'd gulled grew poorer as they sank more and more deeply into the rich morass of their delusions.

There are happier stories, however; like that which concerns the Battle of Irish Bend, near Franklin, Louisiana. When Colonel James Riley was killed, his wife personally rode onto the field in a horse-drawn ambulance, loaded his corpse into it, then carried it off for burial. "She was a woman who was adored by every soldier of the old brigade," Noel claimed with typical enthusiasm; and I am prepared to believe him, discounting his rhetoric only a little, in view of the fact that brigades are composed of too many men for all of them to have the same opinion about anything or anybody, no matter how adorable.

His unfailing gusto notwithstanding, Noel's recall of

such scenes—no matter how touching and comical—is tainted by a pervasive bitterness. Part of this is probably nothing more than the rancorous regretfulness of an old man brooding over his lost youth; but part of it is essentially political, with that special rancour of an old Rebel looking back: "My reader may think that I am radical, but he would not if he had tasted and drank [*sic*] the bitter dregs of that damnable and most bitter cup. *Had the Confederate army been properly officered and supported by a proper, generous and brave government, no army on earth could have conquered it.*" [Italics his.]

There is no truth to such sentimental chauvinism, of course, for from the very beginning the Confederacy was destined to fail. There was no way it could stand up to the overwhelming industrial might and agricultural balance of the northern states, not to mention their great advantage in sheer population to feed soldiers into the Union armies and maintain them with uniforms, food and ordnance for a decade, or however long it might take to suppress the rebellion.

———————

You will have already noticed that Theophilus Noel did not appear to be a shy and retiring man, nor one addicted to self-effacement. Upon those occasions when he suffered seizures of modesty, the reader is caught unaware and momentarily perplexed. Referring to the many wounds he had received in his various battles and engagements, he nevertheless takes pains to confess that they were not nearly so bad as the fear he experienced so often. It's hard to believe he was *excessively* fearful, however, for there are too many examples of bravery in his account.

Furthermore, there are ways of bragging about one's cowardice, and Noel discovered them. By implication, citing instances of our own pusillanimity testifies to our importance. It can also give emphasis to those other occasions when we were heroic. Furthermore, such judgments do not exist in a vacuum; either directly or indirectly, they bear witness to the loftiness and character of those very ideals we possess, against which we are constrained to measure our inadequacies and imperfections. A confession of fear implies that one possesses a standard of heroism against which that fear has been measured.

As for the conventional image of heroism—its recipe requires more than simple bravery. Cleverness and physical prowess must also be added, and we are meant to understand that Noel possessed all three of these ingredients in desirable proportions. For a while he was assigned to the Secret Service, where he was a bearer of dispatches. "In those days," he said, "I was what was termed a runner and there were but few in the army who could walk to keep up with me, and when it came to a long-distance run, no quarter horse could out-travel me."

There was obviously great danger in being a courier, for if he'd been caught by Federal troops with papers on him, his cause would have been betrayed and he would have been shot. He solved this problem by simply memorizing his messages, then upon his safe arrival, writing them down *verbatim.* This was all heady stuff, and heroic enough for an old man to remember, transcribe and publish in a book.

And so it happened. And it would be good to know more about this fiery old warrior with so much of the world stuck in his craw; but from all I could find, there isn't much to learn. Almost forty years before publishing his Autobiography, Noel did write and publish *A Campaign from Santa Fe to the Mississippi . . . A History of the Old Sibley Brigade . . . 1861-1864,* Shreveport, 1865. The first edition is quite rare, and in 1994, a copy was offered by Parker Books of the West, in Santa Fe, for $325. In 1962, Wright Howes listed only three known copies, although a limited edition of 700 copies, edited by Martin Hall and Edwin Davis, was published in Houston in 1961.

Noel seems to have retold the same story in his Auto-biography in his Chapter titled, "Sibley's Retreat from Santa Fe," and from all appearances it is a story worth re-telling. I say "from all appearances" because the editorial seizures and rhetorical smoke are such that they often conceal such pedestrian matters as exactly what's happening, along with where in the hell we are and why in the hell we're there, anyway.

But there's enough to conjecture that Sibley and his group of Texans travelled west to secure the New Mexico Territory for secession, and if necessary engage some of the Federal troops known to be in the region. Much of the action was of the scorched-earth variety, as when they reached Albuquerque and torched six million dollars worth of commisary, quartermaster and medical supplies. Why all of this should have been stored there was not clear, even to Noel and his men. It could have been that they were all too drunk to figure it out. Our author suggests that this was the problem, and then goes on to say that during the campaign, "our commander had never been sober."

The New Mexico adventure, like many others that were far-less deserving, provided Noel with an excuse to tune up his orchestra. "Burning bacon, brandy and whisky and quartermaster's supplies," he wrote, "with the bursting of bombs and the terrific explosion of powder when the magazine was reached. The condition of our army of independent Texans, the majority of whom loved 'red rye,' can better be imagined than I can undertake to describe and explain."

Well, the whole expedition was a disaster. Destroying the supplies in Albuquerque hurt the Confederates more than it did the Federal troops who were dug in some forty miles northeast of Santa Fe. And when eight-hundred men were sent after them, they found General Slough and 6500 hand-picked plainsmen waiting for them at Glorietta Canyon, where they met with a terrible slaughter.

But were they defeated by the enemy that awaited them? Not according to Noel, who claimed that it was booze, not Federal rifles, that did them in. "The three hundred and eighty who had answered their last roll call the day before, whose bodies and bones were left near the mouth of this canyon, were just so many victims who fell in front of General John Barleycorn."

Like most of the stories our hero tells, this one reeks of certitude. No one who had lived as long as he had lived, and had experienced what he'd experienced, could be expected to refrain from having opinions. Certainly not this man.

> And if I had one impression which I could burn on the tablet of the heart of every young man on earth today, it would be this:
>
> Have compassion. Depend only upon what you have to carry you through, and not on the promises of anybody. Keep your money, and it will keep you from all harm. It will make you brave and it will make you honest and it will make you a good citizen, and in old age you will be happy from being able to take care of yourself, ever bearing in mind that as long as you have the bone, the dog will follow you. Drop it, and your bone and dog are both gone. "Weep and you weep alone," but laugh and the world will laugh with you and keep it up all night while you are sound asleep and your interest is growing.

Shades of Polonius and the Robert Frost of "Provide, Provide." Also any number of cynical witnesses of the human species and condition, along with at least one-third of the old English proverb which states that, "With money, Latin and a good horse, you can get through life."

Theophilus Noel's frontispiece portrait in my copy shows a handsome old man with a neatly trimmed white beard, wearing what appears to be a CSA ribbon pinned to his chest. He is frowning, which seems only appropriate, and far more dignified in appearance than one would suppose from the wild and exuberant energy of the writing.

Still, there he is, caught forever at some moment late in his life, shortly after he had founded his own publishing company in Chicago, simply so he could translate his memories onto paper and they could be read by all who could "hear what he had to say" and respond to his loud and vivid fulminations, according to their inclinations, and whoever they might be.

The man who is pictured there wrote a book that might serve as an inspiration for would-be collectors who have despaired at the paucity and high cost of conventionally collectible books. What an adventure it would be to strike out on one's own and start collecting books that are self-published. To create one's own "area" and build a meaningful collection out of books that are generally ignored is an adventure, one that so far as I know, has not been undertaken by anybody—and for good reasons, when one tries to read some of the poetry published by vanity presses. Of course, the fact that I've never heard of anyone collecting self-published books doesn't mean there aren't such people; it's just that I've never heard of them.

One obvious reason that they aren't collectible is that the great majority are simply unreadable. Most are produced by vanity presses, which charge infatuated authors for the printing costs, along with fat profits, deluding them into thinking that there is something absolute in having a book come out under one's own name, and that spending a few thousand dollars is a small price to pay to join the ranks of Jane Austen and Charles Dickens and Henry James.

But there is always that very small portion of self-published books that can prove worthwhile . . . as demonstrated in the present situation, with the surfacing of Theophilus Noel's old book and its providing the occasion for an essay written in service of the fact that this was a man who should not be entirely forgotten, for by all the testimony, he was a cantankerously gifted old cuss, and he is deserving of our attention. We don't always like his testimony, and being as chronocentric as he was, we're not likely to embrace his prejudices; but anybody who wouldn't like his bacon wouldn't know good bacon from leather boots, or a smoke-house from a three-car garage.

4

The Philosophy of the Comma

*H*aving years ago bought a first edition copy of John Stuart Mill's classic *Autobiography*, I recently sat down to read it; but was stopped on the very first page, surprised to notice that its third sentence contains eleven commas. While not utterly extraordinary, such a plenitude of commas in a single sentence is sufficiently uncommon for notice. The sentence was not excessively long, as sentences go; but it was so lacking in grace that its commas stood out like metal studs on a dog collar as it circled in its cumbersome periodicity from beginning to end. If it had been less awkward, I might not have noticed the commas at all; and yet, it was those commas that kept it from flying completely out of control, even as they revealed its ungainliness.

Mill's sentence could hardly be said to belong even as a humble member to the class of extremely unlikely events, a class that includes winning the lottery and being struck by lightning while listening to an opera by Verdi on your portable radio while picnicking. Being struck by lightning is a major event, after all, even for those not immediately affected; and most of us are even interested in the check-out woman—an overweight and impoverished widow with four children, a heavy mortgage on her duplex, and a cat named Frank—who wins nine million dollars in the lottery. We like to contemplate the workings of chance in such events; and it is only proper that we should, for chance is one of the most important, interesting and predictably mysterious factors in our lives.

But we needn't conjure up lightning or fix the lotto, for even within the context of English literary prose, an eleven-comma sentence does not belong to the class of profoundly unlikely happenings. There are far greater comma-stricken sentences, and I will cite a few of them later. But so what? Many would argue that a sentence with an uncommonly large population of commas is a trivial thing for sensible readers to notice, anyway—much less distract them from their reading. No doubt. And yet even *starting* to read Mill's book would strike many of those same people as trivial; which makes ceasing to read it for any reason a quite different sort of thing.

Furthermore, comma counting would seem to be an act of such utter depravity as to verge upon some intellectual equivalent of rape, child abuse or spouse beating. It is earnest fribbling. To count commas is to reveal that one is devoid of imagination on the one hand and seriousness on the other. Comma counting is the act of a scholarly nerd who forfeits any claim to sound judgment along with any respectable system of values. I admit all of this as true; and if I didn't have the mentality of a comma counter, I would be embarrassed.

Nevertheless, there's William Blake's reminder that the road of excess leads to the palace of wisdom—dangerous advice at best, as most sensible people would agree. But roughly translated, what Blake is urging us to do is something like, "Charge on; don't stop now!" Further translated, he is saying something like: "Before dismissing the comma as the very essence of the inessential, let us examine its function and purpose to see if its function and purpose are worth examining."

But you should no longer be kept in suspense about that uncommon sentence containing eleven commas that falls on the very first page of John Stuart Mill's book. The first two sentences express Mill's uneasiness that writing one's autobiography must seem an act of outrageous egotism. Then, after that self-effacing disclaimer obligatory in the personal testimony of a Victorian gentleman, here is the third sentence, containing you-know-how-many of you-know-what:

> But I have thought that in an age in which education, and its improvement, are the subject of more, if not of profounder study than at any former period of English history, it may be useful that there should be some record of an education which was unusual and remarkable, and which, whatever else it may have done, has proved how much more than is commonly supposed may be taught, and well taught, in those early years which, in the common modes of what is called instruction, are little better than wasted.

And there they are—eleven of the little devils. Count them. The sentence itself is not, as I have admitted, one of the glories of English prose. It veers and bounces, and is woefully unsuited for the first page of a book that is widely proclaimed as a classic. It is hardly the product of a man whose I.Q. was once judged to be a marvel of extremity—reaching somewhere above 200, a region where mere humans struggle for air. It is not such a product, that is, if one assumes a direct ratio between I.Q. and an ability to write memorable, prose.[1]

But never mind such questions: they should not detain us. Right now, it's the comma count that counts, and those eleven commas are right there in plain sight for us to contemplate and admire. It must be said that they are all

---

[1] It can be argued that, because of the commas bracketing "and its improvement," the verb "are" in the second line should be singular. It can also be argued that a twelfth comma should follow "profounder"; nevertheless, having mentioned them, I do not want to follow such trails.

correctly used and utterly functional—as reading the sentence aloud will demonstrate—therefore essential for the precise and obviously intended meaning. The third sentence in Mill's *Autobiography* is as clear as it is uninspired. And yet, it contains far more commas than most sentences could tolerate.

But how many commas are proper? Essentially, it's a question of density and definition. Faulkner's long short story "The Bear" is said to have a sentence fifteen hundred words long. Now surely a sentence that long would need a lot of commas. But there is a problem here: can such a lengthy chain of words be legitimately called a "sentence"? If you simply replace periods with commas or semi-colons, does that mean you are actually lengthening a sentence? Hardly, for you're simply changing the mechanics of many sentences, masking them as a single periodicity, shoveling them all into the same vessel.

But there are sentences in modernist, literary texts that shower commas with the largess of dandelions casting their seed. Think of Molly Bloom's interior monologue, or some of the flowing, dream-like sentences in Conrad Aiken's *Ushant*. Such word clusters are sentences, to be sure; but they are sentences in a different mode—they are a sort of non-declarative, incantatory, impressionistic, mumbling discourse that does not play the sentence game the way Henry James or Edith Wharton played it—or John Stuart Mill tried to play it.

Donald Barthelme wrote an entire story consisting of one sentence and with rare lucidity titled it "Sentence." Rich with commas—190 of them—this story was obviously a lot more interesting to write than it is to read. But the legitimacy of the commas in Barthelme's story is still questionable; for how, exactly, can those five pages of text, unrelieved by a single period, be legitimately called a *sentence* ? Calling the story "Sentence" isn't sufficient, because anything can be called anything.

But the charge of not playing the sentence game fairly cannot be made against Mill in the sample quoted. He did not cheat in that sentence. It is clearly a single, recognizable, utterly uninspired sentence in the English language, containing eleven well-placed, sturdily efficient commas. Its lucidity and precision are what one would expect coming out of such a lofty I.Q. And yet, it remains something of a monstrosity, although it is not a monstrosity because of its many commas or the phasing they signal.

In contrast to those non-sentence-sentences of Faulkner and Barthelme referred to, there are real sentences with far more commas than Mill's. Henry James wrote many of that sort. Here is a genuine fourteen-comma sentence—not from the great man's late period, as one might expect—but from a review early in his career of *Eugenie De Guerin's Journal*, by G. S. Trebutien. For the attentive and unhurried reader (the only proper sort for a mindful writer) this sentence is informative and contained; and it reveals its function as a miniature text, as every sentence would if it had the time. Thus, it is worth quoting in all its integrity:

> If Mademoiselle de Guérin, transcribing from the fulness of her affection and her piety her daily record of one of the quietest lives that ever was led by one who had not formally renounced the world, could have foreseen that within a few years after her death, her love, her piety, her character, her daily habits, her household cares, her inmost and freest thoughts, were to be weighed and measured by half the literary critics of Europe and America, she would, doubtless, have found in this fact a miracle more wonderful than any of those to which, in the lives of her favorite saints, she accorded so gracious a belief.

In contrast to Mill's sentence, this is a graceful and accomplished artifact. It is a mini-text, worthy of study. If it does not replace James' entire review, it is nevertheless an integrated text in itself, capable of informing the reader. If you were like me and had never heard of Mademoiselle de Guérin, you emerged from this sentence suitably—in terms of the wordage expended—edified. That sentence is coherent, lucid, mellifluous and balanced. And an essential part of its balance derives from its judicious placement of commas.

As I have hinted, it is surprising to find such a sentence from a work so early in James' career. If readers were to come upon it out of context, they would place it in his mandarin period, sometime after the turn of the century. It's the sort of sentence one would expect to encounter in, say, *The Golden Bowl*, published in 1904. Which suggests the possibility that in his critical prose, at least, James' famously baroque style was more or less with him from the start.

Certainly, it was with him in his last period; and my reference to *The Golden Bowl* was not entirely accidental, for that novel's fourth sentence is a humdinger, an eighteen-comma specimen worthy of anyone who understands that prose can be artful. The book's first three sentences tell us that "the Prince" compares London to Rome, to the latter's disadvantage, and he feels that, paradoxically, London Bridge and Hyde Park are good places to visit in order to sense something of an *Imperium*. Then comes the eighteen comma sentence:

> It was not indeed to either of those places [London Bridge or Hyde Park] that these grounds of his predilection, after all sufficiently vague, had, at the moment we are concerned with him, guided his steps; he had strayed, simply enough, into Bond Street, where his imagination, working at comparatively short range, caused him now and then to stop before a window in which objects massive and lumpish, in silver and gold, in the forms to which

precious stones contribute, or in leather, steel, brass, applied to a hundred uses and abuses, were as tumbled together as if, in the insolence of the Empire, they had been the loot of far-off victories.

It is familiar knowledge that in his old age James dictated his prose to a secretary, scoring it with accents of oral discourse that can be ignored only by speedreaders, and other infidels and heretics, who are willing to read a cheap and easy translation in place of the original. Therefore, since in properly decoding a message we should strive to retain as much as possible of what is originally transmitted, such a sentence as that eighteen-comma monster should be read, not just as it is written, but as it was spoken, vocalized and stressed according to the beat of the commas so meticulously woven into the score.

Are we to assume, then, that James provides one extremity of comma usage? One is tempted to make such an assumption, but to do so would be to forget the resounding periods of past eras when the arts of prose flourished. Think of those great literary marvels of the seventeenth century; think of that venerable old classic, Robert Burton's *The Anatonomy of Melancholy.*

So far, we have ignored a unique feature of commas, a sort of side-usage, in which they are employed in lists to divide terms from one another. (Small clusters of these are woven into the Jamesian texts quoted above.) This listing function is somewhat different from the syntactic role so far, for the most part, under consideration. But lists should not be ignored or scorned, for they are beloved of writers and always have been. In this regard, one immediately thinks of the plenitudinous writers—Whitman, Thomas Wolfe, Henry Miller. Although one immediately thinks of the modern mode, there is nowhere that lists pullulate more extravagantly than in Burton's old classic; and they are enabled to thrive through the intermediation of the comma. Consider this colossal sentence, devoted to the perennial rites of lamentation over human ills and troubles:

> One complains of want, a second of servitude, an-other of a secret or incurable disease; of some defor-mity of body, of some loss, danger, death of friends, shipwreck, persecution, imprisonment, disgrace, re-pulse contumely, calumny, abuse, injury, contempt, ingratitude, unkindness, scoffs, flouts, unfortunate marriage, single life, too many children, no children, false servants, unhappy children, barrenness, ban-ishment, oppression, frustrate hopes and ill success, etc.
>
> *Talia de genere hoc adeo sunt multa, loquacem ut*
> *Delassare valent Fabium:*
> talking Fabius will be tired before he can tell half of them; they are the subject of whole volumes, and shall (some of them) be more opportunely dilated elsewhere.

If you were counting the commas in that splendid monster, you would have come upon thirty-one of them, not to mention two semi-colons, a colon, a set of parentheses, and an indented Latin quotation (which, in typical fashion, Burton obligingly, though loosely, translates after quoting it).

But here, in our study of commas, we are interested in principles, not some scholarly version of a maximum-comma entry in *The Guinness Book of Records*. We are not looking for the most-comma-laden sentence in the English language; or even the one with the greatest density of com-mas, the one with the highest C.Q., or comma quotient . . . the most commas per hundred words, let us say. Surely, one would think, that way madness—or, at least, triviality—lies.

Not that such an inquiry would be entirely useless, and

if we *were* committed to such a quest, we would pause long over a marvelous specimen in Thomas Adolphus Trollope's *What I Remember*. This is on page fifteen of the first American edition of a book of memoirs by Anthony Trollope's older, lesser known (and by every account, including Anthony's own, unjustly favored) brother. The sentence is taken from a copy I bought in a discouraged-looking little bookstore in Fayetteville, North Carolina—within distant earshot of Fort Bragg's rumbling artillery—and it reads as follows:

> And I remember well pondering on the insoluble question why my parents, who evidently, I thought, could, if they chose it, go to the theatre every night of their lives, should abstain from doing so.

While this sentence may not strike casual readers as one possessed of remarkable qualities, they should consider that astonishing cluster of commas beginning with the one following "parents" and contemplate the fact that *it and the four that follow are contained in a single line* (not as quoted but in the original text)! There can hardly be another "non-list" passage in English that is possessed of such a wonderful comma density. One could hardly hope to find another line of text anywhere, consisting of only thirteen words, as this one does, punctuated by five commas.

———————

Many years ago in my youth, already enjoying the pleasures of widely miscellaneous reading, I encountered an interesting theory advanced by some writer whose name I no longer remember. This writer argued that the frequency of semi-colons in a prose text is a clear and accurate measure of the author's intelligence. He did not pause, hedge or equivocate; he stated the matter as categorically as I have done—even *more* categorically than I am doing at this moment, while engaged in this rather fussy, though correctly designed, ancillary clause, consisting of five commas, but without a semi-colon.

Now we know that such a principle is not to be literally believed. We know that we have not been subtly invited to throw semi-colons liberally upon every text in sight (although, if I remember correctly, it's conceivable that my own use of semi-colons increased slightly after I read that). Such a response would be sheer folly, of course; and yet, the semi-colon is truly a supple instrument; and I like to tell my writing students that if a sentence has three or more commas used to divide clauses and phrases, one will likely be sufficiently dominant so as to be replaced by the noble and superbly functional semi-colon.[2]

In *Poetry And Drama*[3] T.S. Eliot expressed something like this—though in different terms—stating that in writing *The Family Reunion*, he paid special attention to the rhythm of the line, deciding that each line should have three stresses, with one caesura and any number of light syllables. In doing so he was attending to the movement within and of the line, asking of the caesura that it organize and balance the line somewhat as a semi-colon organizes and balances the movements within a longer and more complex prose sentence.

The idea behind all this is, of course, the necessity to analyze the line into its natural, speech-governed system of stresses and light syllables. But the line is itself an artifice, which isn't to be scorned, for elsewhere in the same essay, Eliot states that "It is a function of art to give us some perception of an order in life, by imposing an order upon it."[4] So the verse line is merely a "sort of" sentence, the spa-

---

[2] The poetry of Alexander Pope is a rich source of semi-colons; his heroic couplets have an awful propensity toward them at the ends of lines.

[3] Cambridge, Mass., 1951, p. 32.

[4] p. 42.

tial/rhythmic simulacrum of a sentence, which is to say, one periodicity of sensed meaning. This is manifest in every enjambent, where the tension between two sorts of periodicity—the line working against the phrase or clause—is always felt.

But our concern in the present essay is prose; and what needs to be emphasized is the fact that in sentences of twenty or more words there are subtle and intricate balances, and it is a matter of some nicety to score them with the proper notations. This explains the distinct usefulness of commas and semi-colons both—along with parentheses and double-em dashes. In laboring at such distinctions I am relying upon a principle that will be perfectly understood by musicians as well as prose writers.

But it is the comma we are concerned with; and the semi-colon is only *half* comma, the other half being a period. In this respect it is a sort of typographical mule, with the period standing for the mother mare and the comma for the jackass sire. Like all comparisons, however, this is not to be applied too rigorously or too mechanically; the old logicians taught us that we cannot reason from analogy, and they were right—although a lot of good their teaching has done, because it hasn't slowed anyone down, and people still keep on reasoning from analogy as naturally and irresponsibly as they ignore the principles of correct comma usage.

But I should try harder not to be distracted by peripheral and possibly less interesting matters. This is only proper, for the comma is not only a worthy subject, but a majestic one. Its usefulness is very great. It provides a mode for counting the major stresses in a sentence; and the importance of *this* is evident to anyone who has heard an unstressed sentence—the sort of sentence that robots are supposed to speak, if you can believe the more lurid and childish offerings of sci-fi adventures on television.

Although it is hard to think of the comma as at all innovative—after all, it has been around for centuries   it is actually a tool of rather recent and somewhat advanced technology. It seems to have surfaced sometime in the sixteenth century, although the *virgula*, its distant ancestor, had been around for millennia, being familiar to the Romans, as its name signifies.[5]

But when one contemplates the fact that in old manuscripts, words were not even separated until the eighth century A.D., then the comma that we know and use with casual indifference, and occasionally with stunning efficacy, is seen as a relatively modern device for presenting a visual equivalent of that rise and fall of speech essential to rational discourse.

So much is true; and yet, I know a man who has mastered the comma, and claims that when he lectures upon it in his writing classes, the subject does not seem to set his students on fire. He claims he does not sense great excitement among them. The frequency of their psychic vibrations is very low, somewhere in the lower register of the bassoon. He says that students do not come up to him after a lecture, dancing with ecstasy and eager to tell him about a sentence with fourteen commas they remember encountering in a story by Ambrose Bierce, or a nineteen-comma monstrosity lying on page 318 of *David Copperfield*. And he cannot, in all his years of teaching, ever remember a student commenting upon the comma habits of a grandparent.

Being a master of commas, he naturally considers this state of affairs unfortunate. With higher standards of precision in comma usage, he thinks our world would be a better one. Independent of its beauty in modulating the flow and

---

[5] With a root meaning of "a little twig, a small rod, a wand," it was used as an accent mark; one of its medieval progeny, the slant bar ("/"), sometimes indicated a pause (still used to indicate poetic line breaks quoted in a prose text), thus performing one function of the modern comma. This root is evidently *vir*, or "man," which explains why I earlier assigned the semi-colon's comma to the jack ass, leaving the period for the mare.

rhythm of a sentence, the comma is an instrument of logic.[6] Its usefulness in separating an introductory adverb clause from the main clause is especially clear, and should never be omitted, even in those cases where it is deemed inessential.

As for those cases where it *is* essential . . . suppose your subject is Richard Nixon at the time of his resignation from the presidency, and you write the sentence: "When he left Nixon appeared to be a broken man." By omitting a comma after the word *left*, you seem to be speaking of someone leaving *Nixon*, which, though nonsensical in context, is nevertheless utterly grammatical right up to the main verb. Such brief confusion, however, is enough to send readers upon a brief reconnoitering of the territory to sort out the proper relations among the various parts of what should be a lucid and uncomplicated sentence. Readers have better and more interesting things to do than pause over such small though unnecessary confusions.

Verbs which can be either transitive or intransitive cause the trouble in an introductory adverb clause. The winsome and sturdy logic of this rule is so evident, so clear to a head capable of clarity, that you would think it impossible to be ignored. But this is not the case. The professor I have spoken of claims that even sophisticated writers ignore it in great numbers. He says it happens with depressing frequency, claiming that somewhere, at any moment, a writer is busy ignoring it—especially in the United Kingdom, where, for some reason, writers have generally failed to attend to this principle. It occurs to him that writers receive mysterious inoculations that inhibit their abiding by so simple and sensible a convention. He says that there are times when he despairs of ever making people understand, even those who are skilled in other commendable ways. The situation has

---

[6] Indeed, its logicality is an essential part of its beauty, as it signifies a beat in its rhythm; but in this context it is convenient to divide its function clearly and simply between the aesthetic and the rationally utile.

gotten so bad that he tells his students simply to type in two or three hundred commas at the ends of their themes and term papers, and he'll put them where they belong.

All of this notwithstanding, we should strive to be philosophical. The world wags on, and people keep on living their lives, with or without comma awareness. And there is no clear and unmistakable evidence of an increase in the percentage of comma abusers among the general populace. Of course, such a conclusion is necessarily limited to the impressions of one man. And yet, I believe that masters of the comma can immediately see where a comma is lacking, though clearly needed. I would claim that simply by glancing at people it is possible to tell whether or not they are comma abusers.

No doubt the majority will find a preoccupation with commas of little value or significance. Nevertheless, I am convinced that they are wrong in their prejudice, for that is all such opinions reflect. Matters that are worthy or significant can seldom be understood by those who are not experienced in the enterprise of which they are a part. Even though our interest in the comma is not likely to be funded by state or federal agencies, we will continue alone and undeterred. If there were obvious and immediate technological or scientific or economic value in the enterprise of comma usage, we could easily devise a project that would siphon off great riches in the direction of our universities, and, incidentally, ourselves, It has been done elsewhere, in other disciplines, after all; but we know that our labors will never be rewarded in that way.

Understanding the importance of understanding the humble comma is not easy. People everywhere are busy with the things of this world, therefore impatient with theoretical niceties and unlikely to indulge in them. Their ability to understand the significance of comma usage will forever remain seriously limited. If it is argued that the comma relates to clarity of discourse, which everybody admits is important—because when clarity of discourse is lacking, all human relationships begin in confusion . . . if it is argued that commas are essential for the precisions and clarity of discourse—well, no matter how cogent the argument might be as a *theoretical* validity, the immediate problems of the world are too urgent, too demanding and too intolerant for the contemplation of ideal sentence structures. We all know this to be true. After all, we have to be practical, because if we weren't, it wouldn't be practical.

And yet there are times and occasions when I can't help dreaming. Sometimes in my dreams I actually do enter upon a grandiose project of counting every comma of every sentence in all the novels of Thomas Adolphus Trollope's younger brother, Anthony. And then some alert solon in Washington comes across a proposal I've written for a Humanities Grant, and looks hard at it, and then cries out at the triviality of a grown man—a professor at a *university*—wasting the public's money by studying *commas*, for God's sake!

In my imagination, I can almost witness the sustained, skillfully modulated eloquence of that legislator's scorn; and almost witnessing it, I am almost sorry that I will never be able to see and hear such a thing in the real world. I speak of the real world of the latest fashionable truths processed and distributed by the media, the real world of abstract credit and international monetary bureaucracies, the real world of mindless moral posturing and the enduring popularity of cant, the real world of popfizz exploitation of unisex and sexual entropy—not to mention the real world of politics, inhabited by those senators I have invented, who love votes and TV images as much as they despise comma counting. I speak of all *those* real worlds, along with several others that haven't even been thought of yet.

5

A Cabinet of Facts and Follies

*B*ooks are abstractions in which entireties are represented by extracting—which is to say, *ab* stracting—parts to represent their wholes. No matter how voluminous a volume is, and no matter how thorough its treatment, it conveys only a small portion of all that might be said upon its subject, however modest that subject is. Some writers have striven to transcend or escape this limitation, but their attempts were foredoomed. Aiming at comprehensiveness, Joyce created Earwicker's dreamworld in *Finnegan's Wake;* but to the extent that this was literally his purpose, he might as well have tried to eat soup with a fork. When Thomas Hart Benton wrote his political memoirs, *Thirty Years' View* everyone understood that most of what transpired during those three decades was necessarily omitted; if it hadn't been, the book would have required thirty years to read, providing one read at the temporal rate in which the described events were experienced.

If books are abstracts, then reviews of them are abstracts of abstracts. An accurate review provides some sense of what the book is about and how well it has achieved its purpose. Catalogues listing and describing rare books offered for sale at auction, are also "abstracts of abstracts." Such catalogues are familiar to bibliophiles everywhere, and constitute a special literary *genre* of peculiar fascination for those who have eyes to see, and a passion to collect.[1]

Book catalogues are my subject here. Since my familiarity with them is limited to an infinitesimal number abstracted from all those thousands and thousands that have appeared, and since in writing about them, I will select— which is to say, choose or *abstract*—only one of the catalogues in my own small collection, what I write in this small essay will be an abstract of abstracts of abstracts. And if for some reason my essay should be referred to afterwards, that reference will be an abstraction of *it*, adding still another to the series: an abstract of an abstract of an abstract of an abstract. Or, to quote Swift, in his reference to critics: "And these have smaller still to bite 'em, and so it goes, *ad infinitum.*"

Indeed, we spend most of our lives absorbing information in one way or another, and absorbing information means translating it and editing out gibberish, gabble and other irrelevancies—which is to say, it inevitably requires *abstracting*—so that we can remember what we need to know or believe, assuming it will prove useful to our needs and nourishing to our memories. Insofar as these abstractions represent the text, they also translate it. We perform these acts instinctively, unthinkingly, spending our lives winnowing information we find useful or interesting from that which is not. Just as you are now doing in reading this.

In our instinctive lust for originality we tend to assume that the farther down the scale of translations a text is, the more derivitive it is, therefore the less to be cherished, the less "valuable." We collect first editions in response to this

---

[1] The lure of their familiarity is such that it has given rise to the cute neologism "catalog-itis" . . . which is a shame, for the word properly refers to an inflamation of catalogues, not the inflamed imaginaton of the book collector so afflicted. But this is not the only bastardized word in the language; and with luck it will eventually disappear as so many others have done.

instinct, which is not only understandable, but, as many of us would claim, good and healthy. Most collectors are not only committed to honoring the first edition of a valued book, but the first state and first issue, as well. Prices on the rare book market generally measure this preference, to the degree that the first state, first issue, first edition of a collectible book might bring many times the price of a copy into whose bibliographical description the dreaded word "second" has crept.

But interesting things are never that simple, and the proprieties and peculiarities of the rare book market make it as interesting as any market ever known. While the first editions of esteemed titles are generally sought after and valued highly, there are second and later editions that are far more valuable than the first. When this happens it is usually due to substantive additions or revisions, significantly improving the original text; so that the more a subsequent text is edited the more it becomes, in effect, a "first edition *thus*."

Take, for example, Mason Locke Weems's *The Life and Memorable Actions of George Washington*, which was first published in Baltimore in 1800—the year after Washington's death. The 1806 fifth edition, published in Augusta, Georgia, is more valuable, for it is the first in which the wonderful story of George and the cherry tree appears. The irrepressible Weems made up the story to edify his young readers, ironically creating a lie in order to celebrate the honesty of his subject. Not only is the fifth edition of Weems's classic more interesting because of the cherry tree story (which was destined to enter our folklore through the McGuffey Readers), it is rarer and more valuable, for Howes lists five known copies of the first, but only three of the fifth.[2]

---

[2] Wright Howes' *US-iana, NY, 1962.* W-218. (Yes, this is also a 2nd edition—Q.E.D.)

There are other sorts of derivitive texts that rival or even surpass those they are meant to follow or serve . . . somewhat like footnotes that are more interesting than the texts they annotate. Or like the catalogues of dealers in antiquarian books, which might conceivably prove to be as informative and wise as some yet-undiscovered manuscript of Plato containing the *obiter dicta* of Socrates. Indeed, a dull book can be transformed into a virtual masterpiece through the artistry and imagination of a gifted cataloguer.

No doubt it seems fanciful to claim that rare book catalogues are works of art, for most of them are limited by the chance accumulation of rare books over time from various sources; nevertheless, like literary works, they are structures of information; and when the offerings are grand, the bibliophilic passion is stimulated. And if they feature the sale of personal collections or libraries that have been built according to some master plan, they are aesthetically admirable for that reason alone. In this way, their virtues are reflective, deriving essentially from the vision, knowledge and enthusiasm of the collectors who have gathered the books together into meaningful wholes, and not the cataloguer intent upon selling them at their highest value.

While general booksellers' catalogues lack the architectonics of those offering a private library at auction, they can nevertheless prove entertaining and edifying. The spritely description of a book can be possessed of literary merit, just as books promoted and marketed as "great literature" can prove to be worthless. Like trade books, catalogues are instruments of commerce, meant to generate profit; but that doesn't mean that they can't provide what we like to think of as nobler satisfactions, as well. And for a true bibliophile, the distance between the peddling of books and the aesthetic pleasures of collecting is a very short one, for books are like nothing else in the world, and they illuminate all they touch.

Book catalogues are almost as various as the books they offer. Some appear as simple "book lists"—niggardly series of authors and titles and prices, perhaps including a conventional symbol for condition, but otherwise innocent of bibliography. Since bibliographical research is time-consuming and expensive, and requires sophistication, learning and patience, these perfunctory listings are a virtual necessity for titles that are modestly priced in the ten-to-twenty dollar range.

They are, therefore, almost a different species from those elegant productions of that princely class of booksellers that are collectible in themselves. The magisterial dealers of the early 20th century, especially in Great Britain and on the continent, attained to aesthetic and bibliographical heights that have seldom if ever been surpassed; and some of their catalogues are as handsomely bound and printed as the books they celebrate.

Their primary excellence is of course solidly rooted in the quality of their contents, and the accuracy, thoroughness and precision of their bibliographical annotations. At their finest, these mercantile productions designed to sell books at their maximum price are monuments of scholarship. But they also provide a richer, sentimental indulgence, for in their descriptions of antiquarian books they are abstracts and repositories of old times, and reflective of the glories and confusions that have graced and bedeviled the human species throughout history.

They are, in a word, endlessly fascinating—or, in two words, wonderful. To open a book that advertises and annotates books offered for sale fifty or one hundred years ago—most of which were already old at that time—is to step into an enchanted world of antiquarian learning, rich in wisdom and human error, superstition and grandeur. It is to undertake a marvelously entertaining adventure, even as it provides appalling evidence of how limitless and extravagant is the human capacity to believe anything, no matter how exotic and outrageous. It is also to reach back and touch wonders of thought and imagination, conveyed to the present moment through the mercantile processing of antiquarian book dealers long dead. And that processing is, of course, neither more nor less than the act of abstracting, as promised at the beginning of this essay.

One of the finest specimens in my library is Pickering and Chatto's 1902 *Illustrated Catalogue of Old and Rare Books,* a generous quarto bound in sober blue cloth and with its title page featuring the Aldine anchor and dolphin, Manutius's old emblem, signifying *Festina Lente* , or "make haste slowly." Here, however, that motto has been replaced by another, *Aldi Discip Angl,* which is wrapped around the anchor somewhat in the configuration of the dolphin itself. Given the fact that the second two words are obviously abreviations, I assume this would translate as "The English Disciples of Aldus."

The frontispiece is a truly magnificent illumination taken from a 1480 French Book of Hours, *Horae Beatae Mariae Virginis.* It pictures an old man stripped to the waist, sitting with his arms outstretched at his sides and both empty hands palm up, in a gesture eloquent of some combination of entreaty, exhaustion and futility. One would assume that it is Job who is pictured; and his three friends, dressed in the finery of 15th century France, gaze upon him out of expressions that are no doubt meant to convey compassion, but seem equally suggestive of a cold indifference. The referential religious and moral character of the scene has been sacrificed to the aesthetic, for the utter brilliance of the vivid colors, the detailed background, the gilt borders are all splendid. This is something of a technological triumph in a book printed so long ago, reflecting the artistry of the anonymous illuminator so many years before that.

The first item listed for sale in the catalogue is Bishop George Abbott's *A Briefe Discription of the Whole World.* Published in 1634, it is said to contain eighty pages relating to "America, or the New World." With a Riviere binding, this book was priced at two pounds, two shillings. Abbott was Archibishop of Canterbury—a man of whom it was said: "The things that he hath written show him to be a man of parts, learning, vigilance, and unwearied study, though overwhelmed with business."

It is fitting for a book catalogue to begin with a description of the world, for books themselves are microcosms, as they are abstractions; and of course, a book listing books is one that is doubly compressed and intensified—a truth I have already striven cumbersomely to articulate in this essay. Moreover, since the preparation of the Pickering and Chatto catalogue obviously required someone "of parts, learning, vigilence, and unwearied study, though overwhelmed with business," it is only fitting that it should begin by celebrating another such admirable human being.

Africa follows hard upon Abbott, featuring a 1640 book claiming that the inhabitants of Madagascar are "the happiest people in the world"; after which we are immediately treated to wonderful woodcuts showing how the Hottentots catch elephants and fish. This is followed by *The Royal African,* published in 1740, containing the Memoirs of the Young Prince of Annamaboe . . . who "was confided by his father to the captain who sold him."

The section on Americana includes John Frampton's 1596 volume, printed in black letter, titled: *Joyful Newes Out of the New-Found Worlde, Wherein Are Declared the Rare and Singular Virtues of Divers Herbs, Trees, Plantes, Oiles, and Stones.* A section entitled "Of Tobacco and of his great virtues" is said to occupy 25 pages, presumably extolling the medicinal properties of the most famous plant found in this brave new realm. Later entries celebrate the more enduring nostrums produced by the arts of distillation.

Two pages later, Captain Woodes Rogers's 1712 edition of *A Cruising Voyage Round the World* is offered for

2 pounds, 10s. This would have proved a handsome purchase, even at a time when the amount was equal to a ser-
vant's annual salary, because of a section in the book titled: *An Account of Alexander Selkirk's Living Alone Four
Years and Four Months in an Island*—the first appearance
in print of the account that would inspire Daniel DeFoe's
Robinson Crusoe, published just five years later.

And so it goes, page after page, embellished with
quaint woodcuts and containing descriptions of books upon
a marvelous variety of subjects. For example, *A Booke of
Engines,* printed in 1590. The "engines" treated seem im-
possibly quaint by today's standards, for they are of
scarcely any greater sophistication than a garden spade, being "traps to take Polcats, Buzardes, Rattes, Mice and all
other kinds of Vermin and beasts whatsoever."

Then there is a whole school of books about fishing,
including seventeen copies of various early editions of
Isaak Walton's *The Compleat Angler.* And on and on to the
very limits of the imagination. For example, if you're curious about how John Donne looked in his winding sheet—or
was thought to look—you will see a reproduction of the
print, presented in lugubrious detail, from the 1634 edition
of *Death's Duel, or a Consolation to the Soule, Against the
Dying Life and Living Death.*

Donne's image is ghastly enough, to be sure; but there
are other horrors awaiting, such as an illustration from T.
Carey's *The Mirrour Which Flatters Not.*[3] "Dedicated to
their Majesties of Great Britain," we are told, the book is by
Le Sieur de la Serre, Historiographer of France, and it was
translated into English in 1639. The print shows an especially grisly skeleton dressed in a long royal cape and with
its foot placed rakishly upon a globe. The ground seems to

---

[3] I don't know what the "T" stands for; I can't find a "T. Carey" anywhere.
"Thomas Carew" is a tempting thought; but the last letter won't cooperate.

be covered enitirely with skulls, one riding atop an hour glass. Beneath all this there is a passage from Deuteronomy: "O that they were Wise, that they understood this, that they would Consider their latter End."

By now you can see that the entire book is nothing less than an argosy of wonders, teeming with marvels, pictured and written. Most of the titles are 16th and 17th century imprints, and the subjects covered range from dancing to distillation, falconry to fencing, herbals to horsemanship, and magic to monsters. A plate illustrating the last-named shows a small circus of them, displaying a dwarf and a man with two heads. Also shown is a woman with five breasts, demonstrating that not only can there be too much of a good thing, there can be too many.

A rich and various offering of sporting books is followed by forty-eight works by Jonathan Swift, some of which are wonderfully curious. Consider #5379, the 1726 first edition of "*It Cannot Rain But It Pours, or London Strow'd With Rarities, Being an Account of the Arrival of a White Bear at the House of Mr. Ratcliff in Bishopgate Street.*" Then there is reference to *"Faustina,* the celebrated Italian Singing Woman, and of the *Copper Farthing Dean* from Ireland, and lastly of the Wonderful Wild Man call'd Peter."

As for Peter, an enclosed advertisement is intended "To warn all ladies and gentlemen who intend to visit this Wild Man not to carry anything in their pockets that is indecent to prevent accident for the future." I find this inscrutable. The meaning of "indecent" then was simply obscene, just as it is now. So what can such a rune mean? Is the reference to a populace in whom it was common practice to carry indecent objects in their pockets? If so, what *sorts* of indecent objects? Of course we can imagine, but that would reflect us more than the events described. And even if we somehow manage to evoke an image, why would the Wild Boy be more agitated by the sight of it than, say, the average adolescent has always been? And if this mysterious object is in a pocket, how can it be seen, anyway? Finally,what would all this have to do with the *future*? More, that is, than anything else does?

———————

For some, the question that looms over all the preceding is the question of why anyone should seek out such a compendium of marvels in the first place. The information provided by Pickering and Chatto's 1902 Illustrated Catalogue is rich in whimsy, superstition, anecdote and error; but is all that enough to justify possessing, or even *reading* it? A more disciplined and scholarly study might be made from any in the above list of nouns—say, a treatise on the subject of "whimsy" or "superstition." You can almost see their titles as they would appear in another sort of catalogue: *The History of Whimsy in Irish Folklore,* perhaps; or *The Role of Superstition in 18th Century Medicine.* No doubt there have already been books written on those subjects, perhaps with identical titles.

But leafing through the miscellaneous entries of a catalogue like this—no matter how scholarly their annotations—is in itself an act of idleness. Compared to playing golf or tennis, such idle excursions might be said to lack even the rigor of serious entertainment. And yet, many people—I among them—have a special fondness for entertainments that edify as they amuse. To put it crudely, we like our amusements to be "educational." We enjoy being instructed as well as entertained by a good mystective novel, for example. But is there anything like profit in scanning the prints and text of Pickering and Chatto's old catalogue?

Well, there is and there isn't. In John D. Macdonald's color-coded Travis McGee novels, there is a professorial economist named simply "Meyer" who often lectures McGee learnedly on various subjects, courteously enabling the reader to listen in and profit from the playful expenditure of so much wit and erudition. But McGee himself is not above (or below) lecturing; and here, too, the reader delights in so much information conveyed so vividly and well. In short, much of the enduring popularity of the Travis McGee novels derives from so much intelligence packed into the sugar pills of story telling.

But what is an old book catalogue in contrast to such excellent examples as John D. Macdonald's novels? One might as well read a book catalogue for plot as for sustained discourse of any sort. And yet, there is another sort of witnessing here, and it seems to me utterly worthy of our time— not in the sense that it will edify us in specific ways, or add to "professional" knowledge, whatever that might be; but in the sense that it provides the unique pleasures of expanding our sense of the limits and varieties of the human condition; and in doing so, bears witness to things worth knowing.

What things? First of all, the marvelously various ways in which people in the past have tried to cope with life. It is generally, rather than specifically, edifying for us to read the titles and annotations of old and obscure books because they are imprints of old beliefs, old nostrums, old fears and fascinations, old interests. And while there are many things that we as individuals may find uninteresting, our indifference seldom extends to those who do somehow manage to be fascinated by those very same things. Interest generates interest, and interested people are interesting. I don't have any particular feel for golf or horses or balloon travel; but how could I be immune to the passion of those who do find those subjects delightful?

This is a variation upon the venerable humanistic argument, of course, and it is to some extent implicit in most college-level "course offerings" in philosophy and history and literature. Reading an old book catalogue is not entirely different from taking a survey course in a subject one does not expect to pursue seriously. An academic policy designed to satisfy distribution requirements is sometimes referred to as a "cafeteria" or "smorgasbørd" curriculum; and one can see why, for it rests upon sadly limited and highly questionable pedagogical assumptions. Having said that, however, one must admit that nobody seems to be able to come up with anything better for introducing young people to the vast and rich heterogeneities of the human adventure.

As instruments of instruction, old book catalogues will hardly serve any specific curricular purpose. Although it's possible to conceive of courses with such titles as *Rare Book Catalogues, Past and Present* or *Rare Book Catalogues: An Index to Entropy,* it would be something of a challenge to establish a linear sequence of courses, complete with prerequisites and an ordered progress toward more and more specialized and difficult phases of a specific subject. But such a limitation has less to do with knowledge itself than with its taxonomies—specifically, those taxonomies essential for the convenient structuring of professional expertise and university curricula.

If not essentially random in their contents, rare book catalogues are nevertheless unique productions, full of oddities and error, and therefore exquisitely representative of our humanity. The fact that the titles offered are arranged alphabetically is interesting, for the alphabet is a basic and natural basis for taxonomy. The Greeks of the classical age understood this, thinking of the basic units of the physical world as *stoicheia*, or the letters of the alphabet.

And, indeed, we still think like this, even when we think we don't. The habitude is so simple and effective and so deeply ingrained in the way we organize information that it's not surprising that it has come to seem natural. Still, all of our organizational modes are transactionals, after all. You can't have organization unless there's something unorganized, or disorganized, to work with. Without chaos, there's not only no *reason* for order, there's no point to it.

And it is in this that we find the source of the attraction. As instruments of order, books are dependent upon chaos and confusion. It is not their design alone that fascinates and beguiles us; it is their design in tension against the ignorance and folly and wild plenitude they are meant to domesticate. And where is this better represented than in a catalogue that has gathered from the centuries an assortment of old and out-dated books, often jostling in wild irrelevance to one another, jammed into their slots by the arbitrary rule of the alphabet? And when one considers the dark multitudes of events behind and implicit in each title, such plenitude is manifest in all its glory.

The mystery of time can to some extent be conveyed by two simple models: the linear and the growing circle.[4] Both are commonsense representations, and to that extent useful. And both convey a sense of the relentlessly increasing distance from past events as we travel forward in time. The linear in the sense that in temporal progression a point, 15, will be farther than a point, 9, from a point, 4; and so on. The growing circle model complicates this movement, in that all points move centrifugally in time. On a growing circle, a point at two o'clock not only departs linearly from the inner points on its own arc, but it increasingly deviates from the points at one and three o'clock on the expanding circumference.

The usefulness of this model is obvious in the context of specialization: the career of, say, an 18th century literary scholar will grow more and more eccentric with reference to scholars of Victorian literature and Restoration drama. To consider the matter nicely, scholars whose specialty is, say, Fielding, will find their careers relentlessly, though less noticeably, diverging from those whose specialties are DeFoe or Boswell.[5] Our two-o'clock scholar's growing career

---

[4] A third model is the sphere; but, for all its potential usefulness, dealing with it would prove far too complicated for our present purpose.

[5] The changes in the growth of a discipline have three basic sources: the inevitable accumulation of "new" information; one's own individually growing perspective in the field; and the interactions between scholars in the old ceremony of "book talking to book."

will, of course, grow in still more radically deviant directions relative to the physicist engaged in small particle research or the historian of macro-economic phase patterns in
the distribution of consumer goods in developing countries.

Because of the specialization that inhibits and impris-
ons all of us to one degree or other, we have a recurrent
need to get in touch with our sense of the wonderful variety
of things. The world is greater than our specialized knowledge dreams possible. We'll never be able to escape the alphabet, or some similar organizational mode; but we can
use it to see beyond, utilizing it in its role as the basic symbol, out of which all knowledge grows. This knowledge is
as old as the Greeks referred to earlier, in their utilization of
the *stoicheia* of the alphabet for symbolizing the elements
of the physical world.

The native habitat of the alphabet is the book, of
course; and the book of books is a rare book catalogue. It is
not our only access to the plenitude of life; there is the daily
newspaper, of course. But the newspaper is largely focused
upon the present moment, whereas old book catalogues
teem with things that were once judged to be true and relevant, but are now mostly forgotten.

Who could remain indifferent to them? Hamlet said
that we are creatures "large in discourse, looking before and
after." It is a curious statement, for either of the two adverbs
can refer equally to the past or the future, depending upon
whether our attention is focused within the subject or without. But however it's done, there is an unmistakeable challenge in it that we should look into our past. Without doing
so, our discourse is diminished . . . and through that diminu-
tion, our lives.

Think of the Past as it can be seen through various
windows, and think of how many of us are frenetically intent upon only the present moment, or its tyrannically dominant fixation upon the imminent future. Think of some

window through which one might pause and look to see where we've been and what we've done. . . . which is to say, what we are, for we are made of the past, and without memory we cannot exist.

One such window is the 1902 Pickering and Chatto *Illustrated Catalogue of Old and Rare Books*. Marvels are to be discovered in such a place, and those marvels will tell you something of what we have been, and what we are and what we might be.

6

Vesalius and the Sleepy Oncologist

With the passage of years, medical and legal books fall into a limbo where they're too old for relevance and too new for antiquarian inerest. And yet, just as the unbaptized righteous were once supposed to be redeemed from their temporary oblivion by the passage of time, and just as time is still widely believed to be a cure for many of our earthly misfortunes . . . so does the passing of years eventually salvage old books from their limbo of neglect. Generally, the older an old volume gets, the more interesting and "collectible" it becomes.

I remember a conversation with an oncologist on a crowded flight to Minneapolis many years ago. I was sitting in a window seat and he was in the aisle seat beside me. Eventually, surfacing from a shared state of stultified boredom, the two of us struck up a conversation, desperate for any excuse to stay awake. We began by trading reasons for travelling: he planned to attend a conference at the Mayo Clinic, and I was headed for a campus visit at Gustavus Adolphus College, some seventy miles away in St. Peter, where I had been invited to give a talk and read from my fiction.

He accepted this calmly enough; but when I mentioned that I intended to spend the night in Minneapolis so I could visit several local antiquarian book dealers the next morning, he came fully awake and expressed astonishment. His incomprehension verged upon indignation; he seemed personally offended by the notion. Why in the hell would any sensible person waste time by going in search of old books?

With that question, the battle was engaged; those sitting around us on the plane might have been able to hear the beating of drums and blare of trumpets. It was lovely. By now, both of us were wide-awake. It was obvious that he was the sort who took as much pleasure from argument as I did. This was before the days of in-flight movies; but even if they'd been available, the promise of our disagreement might well have eclipsed a rerun of *The Sands of Iwo Jima* or *Ma and Pa Kettle Go To Town*.

I was, of course, aware of a certain advantage: this man obviously had strong feelings about the issue; his antagonism gave me much more to work with than a tepid indifference. Already, I sensed an interesting complication in the mustering of his forces in the gathering storm of axiological battle—perhaps a history of previous debate and rehearsal in his own mind. Some of his troops might have been ready to desert to my side if I could only find the rhetorical means to inspire them with rebellion.

But such means eluded me, and my arguments had little effect on his sullen, stubborn—though vociferous—prejudice against the very idea of collecting old and rare books. So finally, after an exchange of mutually insulting, though politely encoded, references to our respective qualities of mind, I resorted to another sort of rhetoric, and in a tone of exasperated tolerance for his mulishness, I said, "Come on, now, be honest—wouldn't you *really* like to own a first edition of Vesalius?" To which question, he paused only briefly, then nodded and said, "Yes."

I interpreted this admission as his complete and utter capitulation; although it could be that he was simply tired of the argument, or felt it had lasted long enough, for the seatbelt lights had gone on and our plane was beginning to circle for a landing.

Recently I phoned to purchase a single 18th century manuscript leaf promising a cure for dog bite. It was advertised in a catalogue issued by Roger Bertoia, of The Bishop of Books, in Steubenville, Ohio—a small city on the Ohio River, famous as the birthplace of Dean Martin, and memorable as that of Dard Hunter, the great and scholarly expert on old paper making. When the document arrived several days later, it was accompanied by a note from Roger saying that my phone order had been the first of five he had received in swift succession for this small and rather quirky item. The sheet upon which the "Receipt" is written has a dime-sized hole in it, and the ink of the handwriting is badly faded. But it is mostly legible and intact, and reads as follows:

> To Cure the bite of a mad Dog take an herb that grows in wet land mostly to be found at the outlets of swamps it has a square stalk Notched leaf in Read at the Root a purple bloom and the Pod containing the Seed is in the shape of a bell.
>
> It must be gathered before or after Dogs Days and kept out of the Sun.
>
> Take of said Herb and cut it up fine and make a tea as strong as Common Tea.
>
> Give to a Child of three years old one gill night or morning fasting.
>
> To a child of 8 years old 1 1/2 gills night and morning.
>
> To a child 12 yrs old 2 Do_____Do_____Do
>
> To an adult 2 gills night and morning.
>
> The patient must refrain from butter or anything of a Greasy Nature in his diet and must drink no Spiritous liquors. The above must be given two Days Successively & then miss one day. & should

that day that is missed, he must take a Portion of B
[   ] sulpher Sufficient to Purge him & through
the Whole process must be very Carefull of wetting
his feet as that is very pernicious.

and for Curing the Rheumatism or gout the patient must take a double portion of the tea and as
much Sulpher as will Purge the 3rd day & be careful
of wet feet also.

NB the tea for Cannine madness must be continued forty days that is two days the medicine & the 3
day the Sulpher.

There are several interesting things about this old remedy. My Ohio University colleague, Professor of Biology,
Ivan K. Smith, informs me that the plant referred to is almost
certainly the *Scutellaria Lateriflora,* or "mad dog skullcap,"
a non-aromatic member of the mint family. In the 18th century this plant was generally thought to be a cure for rabies,
but it was eventually found to be worthless for that purpose,
although even today some people continue to use it as an
herbal sedative.

There is a signature on the back of my sheet, in two
places and in the same hand: "John P. Turney, Weston, Fair-
field, Conn." Given the fact that Turney is not a famous figure, this does not seem particularly significant; but its being
an "Americana" item is important, for a stubborn insularity
is almost universal among book collectors, no matter how
cosmopolitan and sophisticated they are in other ways; and
for an American, the difference between an old Connecticut
document with a home remedy for dog bite and one from,
say, England, is a meaningful one.[1]

A further curiosity is the added information, given almost as an afterthought, that this potion is also effective in
curing the rheumatism and gout—far more common than

---

[1] Here I labored to somehow work in Noel Coward's "mad dogs and English-
men go out in the midday sun"; but my esemplastic gifts failed me. Except for
this footnote—which is, of course, cheating.

rabies, then as well as now. Given such a casual and dismissive reference, one wonders if maybe the herb's possible usefulness in curing bursitis, gangrene and swamp fever had been unaccountably left out. But the document is strangely silent about these, possibly because there was no more room at the bottom of the sheet . . . although more probably because such outlandish notions had mercifully escaped the teeming brain of the author responsible for this nostrum.

The interest of old prescriptions of this sort has little to do with their therapeutic usefulness; they open a small window upon worlds that are hauntingly strange to us, yet somehow familiar. We find it peculiar that our grandparents to the seventh, eighth and ninth generations took such nonsense seriously and yet somehow managed to survive long enough to reproduce their kind and help perpetuate the pharmaceutical beliefs of the day.

Viewed in retrospect from these more sanitary times, the mere fact of their survival seems an impressive achievement. Outliving the ministrations of doctors who were often ill-educated, and addicted to cupping, leeching, bleeding and dispensing drugs of uncertain composition and proportion is remarkable. But it helps explain why quaint old documents of this sort, along with the many published volumes that are often just as colorful and every bit as unsophisticated, are so popular among collectors, especially professionals in medicine.

Although a fictional character, the narrator of Robertson Davies' novel, *The Cunning Man*[2], is such a physician. In writing about his schooldays, Dr. Jonathan Hullah remembers when he first became interested in book collecting. Mr. Ramsay, the head history master and an authority on the saint lore of the Middle Ages, had been invited to talk to their club, and he showed the boys his personal copy of William Morris's 1892 edition of Caxton's *The Golden*

---

[2] (NY, 1994)

Legend. Appropriately, young Hullah's first glimpse of the book was itself something of a religious experience.

As an old man, Hullah remembers how he and a schoolchum used to raid the old bookstores in Toronto. "I bought old medical books," he said, "stuff discarded by students in the nineteenth century, not because I thought they could teach me anything of value about modern medicine, but because they contained interesting clues to the medical past."[3]

This is nothing but sound common sense, of course; although the disclaimer that they could not teach him anything about modern medicine is questionable, for the growth of knowledge is not linear, but cyclical—with manifold variations—and the future is often created by plundering the past for inspiration and ideas. Indeed, Hullah himself had been privileged to witness an instance of this as a young boy in the wilds of Ontario, where he watched an old Ojibwa medicine woman with the wonderful name of "Mrs. Smoke" treat wounds with bread mold, decades before the discovery of penicillin.

So the Past is a treasure trove waiting to be raided to inspire, illuminate and even help us devise the future. All true; and yet, its worth is not confined to an exiguous utilitarian function; it is not only a means to an end, but an end in itself. As Hullah says: "Mr. Ramsay introduced us to the beauty of the printed book, which comparatively few people understand, and which has in my time become the concern of small private presses. Faced with that Morris *Golden Legend* I fell in love, in one of the few really rewarding romances of my life: I fell in love with beautiful books, and now, as an old man, I have a harem which is by no means trivial."[4]

To argue that books are possessed of a beauty that few

---

[3] NY, 1995. P. 74.
[4] Ibid. Same page.

people can understand is a bold claim, and, like all aesthetic principles, essentially elitist. The issue is no different from the belief that few people can be said to understand, with any pretense of sophistication, Bach's music or Rembrandt's paintings. Like any serious aesthetic principle, such a claim of privilege cannot be disproved, it can only be disagreed with. And to paraphrase and extend the application of the venerable legal axiom, such a declaration is innocent of insignificance until proven insignificant.

Beauty and referential meaning are not discrete values, of course: the beauty books possess could not exist without the implicit promise of the covert mystery they are devised to protect—that "reading matter" which is not matter at all, but spirit. Books are interior instruments, whose exteriors betoken and symbolize that which is within, thereby not simply justifying, but deserving elegance in their integument.

As age is intrinsic to the beauty of many sorts of books, it is part of the fascination of old medical documents glamorous with error. This helps explain those five phone calls in response to Roger Bertoia's catalogue advertising an old handwritten sheet promising a cure for rabies that no modern reader, physician or lay person, could take seriously.

One's relationship with the Past is everywhere a crucial one, but it is always somewhat ambiguous. From what is known about him, there was a 16th century anatomist who exemplified this ambiguity in his writings. I am, of course, referring to Vesalius, one of the great figures in the long and complex history of medicine.

My reference to him in my argument with the sleepy oncologist on the flight to Minneapolis was not informed. Vesalius was little more than a name to me, along with some vague images remaining from the anatomical illustra-

tions of the human body I had seen in various reproduc-
tions. It is possible that my antagonist had no more vivid
knowledge of the great man; but such ignorance could only
add power to the reference, for vague images are not only
tolerant of legends, they are sympathetic to them.

But what of Vesalius's own relationship with the Past?
It appears to have been interestingly ambivalent, for he was
critical of his predecessors *not* for being old-fashioned, but
for not being old-fashioned enough. He disapproved of
their neglecting their own Past. Specifically, he was referring to the work of Galen, "The Prince of Physicians," who
had by Vesalius's century already dominated medical theory for thirteen hundred years. The paradox is inescapable:
Vesalius, the great anatomist who by his intensive and un-
prejudiced study of the human body liberated so much
anatomical theory from error, found fault with those who
had preceded him for not attending to those very ancient
texts which were the source of so many of those very errors.

Things are never really that simple, however. Truth
and error can seldom be found as discrete values stamped
upon ideas; they are often beautifully and intricately
whorled together, like designs in old marble. And it was
Vesalius who noted with approval that the practical
anatomy taught by his predecessors was based upon their
studies of the lower animals. Even so, he repudiated
Galen's brain anatomy for this very reason—that it was *too
closely* based upon his study of the brains of the lower animals. The influential devolution of ideas is a very complicated issue, as it should be; but it is gratifying to detect in
all this confusion clear prints of influence, such as prefigu-
rations of the theory of evolution deeply ingrained in the
study of the centuries'-old practice of studying human
anatomy by refering to the lower animals.

What sort of man was Vesalius? His remarkable gifts
were early manifest in his youth, and these gifts were such
that he became legendary even in his lifetime. Being legendary, he inspired legendary stories, some of which were

not entirely to his credit . . . such as the rumor that his curiosity about arterial function was so obsessive and passionate that he actually cut into living bodies to better understand how blood circulates. Whatever the truth of those reports about his own curiosity, it is known that he aroused the curiosity of the ecclesiastical authorities, for he was found guilty of impiety, whereupon he was sentenced to make a pilgrimage to Jerusalem in order to expiate his guilt.

Again and again in his writings, Vesalius refers to Galen, physician to three Roman emperors and said to be the author of over five hundred books. Vesalius's preoccupation with him is indicative of the magisterial influence of the old Roman's teachings up to the time of Vesalius, himself, who more than any other anatomist was responsible for displacing them.

But Galen's observations were half the source of his own displacement as the master of anatomy; the other half was, of course, nature. And yet, nature is never untroubled by the mind that regards it, and in his dethronement of the Prince of Anatomists, Vesalius is attentive to this complexity. He everywhere expresses reluctance to disagree with his great predecessor, even though he is finally compelled to do so simply because of the irrefutable testimony of what he sees.

He is even sympathetic to those physicians whose very training prompts them to defend Galen, in spite of what their own eyes tell them. And yet, he could understand that there was no turning back. "Even they," he wrote, "influenced by the love of truth, have little by little given way and shifted their faith from his masterful teachings to what their eyes and reason proclaim to be true."

This is by now an old story conveying an old truth, as old as the first stirring of the scientific spirit, and its relevance is still with us and still problematical. And it is still very complex, for where but from the Past do the perceptions and reason that repudiate the Past come? We are born into a world of language, and most of the language is old and stubborn and insidiously influential, even as it is the ground of genius and the future. In his *The Parliament of Foules*, Chaucer wrote:

> For out of olde feldes as men saith
> Cometh all this new corne fro yeer to yere,
> And out of olde Bokes, in good feyth
> Cometh al this newe science that men lere.

As it is difficult to measure the degrees of influence in the history of ideas, so it is difficult to assess the genius of such early figures as Vesalius who seemed to tower above their contemporaries. But we can be sure that to some extent their remarkable statures are illusive, for—to adapt a famous phrase from St. Augustine—we are all aswim in the Past that is past and the Past that is present and encoded in those around us. And just as Vesalius was inspired by Galen, he was influenced by all of those around him, for even their errors were useful in stimulating and challenging him to understand them and demonstrate their mistakes.

"Contradiction," Hegel said, "is the power that moves things." It is certainly at the heart of dialectic, the democratic political process and trial by jury, as conceived in the centuries-old tradition of Anglo-Saxon law . . . not to mention almost every story worth telling. And it is manifest in unlikely contexts, such as two sleepy and opinionated men on a plane flying to Minneapolis who get into an argument about the good sense implicit in collecting old and rare books—an argument more obviously about the Past than most arguments.

Since Vesalius may be said to have won that argument, it seems only felicitous to evoke his memory once again. He once claimed that at its simplest, medicine is the addition to the body of what it lacks and the purging of its superfluities. If one were to add "errors" to superfluities, the formula could be applied to far more than medicine, as it is narrowly conceived. For as this is true of the body, it is also true of the way we metabolize time and information, purging the Present time from past mistakes, and then trying to determine what is lacking so that it can be added. And yet, much of what is added will also be found to come from the Past, in one of its guises, in some version or other. Where else could it come from?[5]

We find the Past in the visual beauty of the printed page, and it is from this vessel that we drink in the world. And yet, there is more than seeing at work, because the sounds of speech are mysteriously encoded in the typography. This embodiment is, after all, the genius of books. And it is profoundly mysterious, for how can the spoken word be embodied in print? How, exactly, do signs on the page evoke the human voice? How is it that we can hear what is written? What enigmatic metamorphosis is contained in such a casual, commonplace act as reading these words you are now reading?

These turn upon an old issue, to be sure. Vesalius, himself, was perplexed by it—although in a far-more literal sense, for near the end of his life, he stated that what had most eluded his understanding was the mystery of the human ear. We know of his perplexity because we can hear it in the words he wrote, words that have been printed on paper, over and over again, in all the copies of all the old and rare editions that have carried his voice down through the centuries.

---

[5] There is, of course, an answer to this ostensibly rhetorical question: to "come from" something is a statement of cause and effect, and whatever randomness there might be in the universe is by definition uncaused. But such a nice distinction would be inappropriate in the present context—except, perhaps, as a footnote.

7

Heraclitus On Hog Island

T hat the fetish of fine condition has troubled book collectors for centuries is manifest to all bibliophiles, with the possible exception of those who object to the word "fetish." Most would agree that mint or nearly mint condition—including dust jackets, of course— is desirable when buying modern first editions for one's personal library; and to a great extent, the criterion of fine condition applies to antiquarian books, as well.

"To a great extent," but not entirely. It can be argued that the patina of age enhances an antiquarian book precisely as it does an Empire bureau or Sheraton desk. If the dull gloss and rubbed-smooth corners of finely worked cherry or walnut furniture are possessed of a unique beauty because of their witnessing to having survived the slow, relentless work of usage and time, why should not signs of wear in old books bound in leather or buckram be similarly honored?

No reason at all. And yet, while some collectors might find such an aesthetics agreeable, a greater number ignore its good sense and tolerate copies in poor condition only grudgingly and as a desperate necessity. If a volume is so breathtakingly scarce that another copy is unlikely to turn up at any time, at any price, should it be spurned simply because it is in shabby condition? Suppose one were to come upon a copy of one of the two eighteenth century editions of Zadok Cramer's *Navigator* that Wright Howes cited as having been published in Pittsburgh, although he knew of no surviving copy[1]; are we to believe that any sensible collector would ignore a copy if it surfaced in some book shop, attic or barn, simply because it was worn, tattered and grubby?

Hardly. But the hypothesis becomes even more dramatic if the book is incomplete, lacking maps or perhaps significant portions of the text. Or even the "obligatory" title page. Here we are faced with a whole new level of imperfection, compounding deficiencies with blemishes and adding to the horror of all right-thinking bibliophiles locked inside their rigid proprieties.

The notions I'm advancing aren't quite as heretical as they may seem. While the solander case was originally devised to protect botanical specimens in the British Museum, it was eventually adapted for housing old books, and it has since done so to protect those that are quite valuable, while concealing their imperfections. My first edition of Emerson's *Poems, NY, 1847*, is encased in a handsome maroon solander, protecting a worn copy in drab green cloth and with a broken hinge. I paid an Atlanta dealer $200 for this in 1980, and fifteen years later, Ahearn listed it at only $1000. Furthermore, that would be for a copy in fine condition, while mine is not.

And yet the solander case is itself attractive, both as an artifact and as a symbol of respect for the book as a classic early work of the Sage of Concord. Here the question is: would my tattered and worn copy have been worth more if it had been handsomely rebound instead of encased in a solander box? I don't know; but I think not; and my own feeling about the matter is clear: I like it the way I found it; if I hadn't, I wouldn't have bought it. And I still feel this way; which is what matters.

---

[1] That was in 1962, of course; if a copy has turned up since then, I don't know about it.

My reference to Zadok Cramer's *Navigator* relates indirectly to a defective copy of its sixth edition, published in Pittsburgh in 1808, which I bought from an antique dealer in Chillicothe, Ohio, a few years ago. I had come upon this disgustingly worn and battered little book a year or so before that, but reluctantly passed it by because of its condition, along with the fact that it was missing its title page. No bibliophile with the least pretense for possessing standards and good taste would have given it a second glance.

But *I* did. And then a third. And after leaving the shop, I kept thinking about it. What's a title page, after all? Only the most important leaf in a book, so far as *collecting* is concerned. Sure. But didn't the rest of the book seem to be more or less intact? It's true that the pages were numbed and softened by the years, and that some of the print was as pale as cobwebs; but otherwise the book seemed to be intact. And on page 72 wasn't the legend, "Falls of the Ohio," printed in black letter Gothic? This was a wonderful anachronism, connecting a shabby little book printed on the American frontier with the 1611 King James translation of the Bible and the first folios of Shakespeare!

The woman who owned the antique shop had priced *The Navigator* at $75.00, another good reason for passing it by. But I kept thinking about it. I couldn't get it out of my mind. I kept reminding myself that the sins of omission are far worse than those of mere blundering and folly committed in the name of purpose. So I finally gave in, and my wife and I drove the sixty miles to Chillicothe, where we found that the price of the book was now $95.00. Surprise. But I bought the damned thing anyway, with scarcely a grumble, for I wasn't about to create a scene or let the book remain there in the shop, where someone else might buy it. If I did, it would haunt me forever in its absence.

This book is one of the famous series of guidebooks Zadok Cramer brought out to help flatboatmen and keelboatmen (and, later, steamboatmen) negotiate their way safely down the tricky, winding and dangerous channels of the Ohio River, which was for much of the 19th century the single great passageway to the West. Because of rapidly accumulating information about the river, along with the changes in the landmarks and channels, *The Navigator* was often revised and reprinted under different titles, some editions separated by only a year.

I covet this little book for a reason other than its intrinsic interest, however. Years ago I had bought a copy of the 1837 edition, by then titled *The Western Pilot*, and listed as written by Samuel Cummings. Actually, the scoundrel "Cumings" (as his name was sometimes spelled) had simply pirated and edited Cramer's *Navigator* for his own purposes, bringing out twenty editions under different titles from 1825 to 1866.

Like its prototype, Cummings's 1837 edition is not confined to the Ohio, but includes text and maps of the Mississippi, along with references to the Missouri, Ozark and other western rivers. Appended to the later edition are "Extracts from the Life of Daniel Boone" (not further identified); while the 1808 edition reprinted part of Patrick Gass's journal of the Lewis and Clark expedition—Gass's book being the first about that great adventure, and published the previous year, right there in Pittsburgh.

I had written about my 1837 copy in an essay titled, "The Wear of Time," published in *Booking In The Heartland* in 1986,[2] making very much the same argument about condition as I have just done. But now I wanted to compare the two editions. Since they had appeared a generation apart, their differences can be seen as one measure of the years that separated them . . . even though from our perspective, one might expect those differences to prove negligible, the way fence posts seem close together from the distance of a quarter mile. Sure, but try to spit from one post to the next.

---

[2] Johns Hopkins University Press.

Not only did the old guide book grow and change in response to the accumulating information about the river and the needs of riverboatmen, but the nomenclature of the river, and even the river itself, changed. In short, what did Cummings decide to include and what omit from the material he stole from Cramer? What information was retained and how was it altered? And how much new information was added?

These differences are immediately apparent in comparing the two volumes. The 1808 edition starts out reading almost like a modern tour guide, with leisurely descriptions of the towns and scenery and other sights along the river. Its opening pages are chattier, and more interested in local color than those of the later edition. For example, Pittsburgh is described in detail for the benefit of eastern travelers and immigrants:

> Upon entering the town, the stranger is rather offended with its dark and heavy appearance. This arises from the smoke of the coal, which is used as the common fuel, and of which about 170,000 bushels are consumed annually. It costs six cents a bushel at your door, and is said to be equal to any in the world. Our rough hills are filled with it, and our rooms in winter feel the effects of its warmth, and cheerfulness.

There is a certain wistful comfort in realizing that air pollution is not a modern invention, and that even in 1808 people knew how to blacken and poison the air. It appears that Pittsburgh, up until World War II known as the "Smoky City," had been working at its reputation for almost a century and a half, and was busy perfecting it even before Nicholas Roosevelt's first steamboat headed for New Orleans. Our heritage of urban pollution was well-begun in an age when doctors still bled their patients, and whiskey was used as currency.

In contrast to the earlier one, the opening of the 1837 edition is business-like and practical. The smoke of Pittsburgh was ignored as not worthy of notice. Indeed, there is hardly any reference to the city itself. Like the city, *The Western Pilot* had grown larger. Even so, this later edition seems to give less attention to local color and details of regional interest, suggesting a shift in purpose. The 1808 book was calculated to lure people from the East to cross the Alleghenies and settle in Pittsburgh . . . or at least use it as a port of embarcation. The later edition, however, reflects less need for luring immigrants westward, since they're already jamming the roads and trails; instead, it is focused more upon the exigencies of getting downriver safely and quickly, with as little fuss and trouble as possible. And, of course, much of this shift reflects a greater and more detailed knowledge of the river. There was a lot more information available in 1837 than in 1808, and even a larger book had less room for literary indulgence and stylistic embellishment.

Like those of 1837, the entries of the earlier edition are interspersed with maps of the river. On page 40, after the introductory material, the working text is announced as follows:

OF THE OHIO RIVER.
ITS CHANNELS, RIPPLES, ISLANDS,
SAND-BARS, RIVERS, CREEKS, TOWNS,
DISTANCES FROM PLACE TO PLACE, &c.

WITH CORRECT MAPS.
ON shoving off at Pittsburgh, if the water be high, your boat requires but little attention; if low, to avoid grounding, you must before you get quite opposite the Point, begin to pull over towards the left shore, going between the end of the Monongahela bar, and one made by the entrance of the Allegheny.
(See MAP 1, page 42.)

No. 1, Hamilon's island,
This island is about one mile long, and is now the property and residence of Doctor Brunot, a French gentleman of much taste in agriculture and horticulture, skilled in the practice of physic, and celebrated for his open and general hospitality to strangers and friends.

Not only does the 1837 edition lack the chatty warmth of the above description, it does not show a "Hamilton's Island" at all; it lists it as "Brunot's Island," however—placing it $2\frac{1}{2}$ miles from the Pittsburgh wharf, but giving no information about the French doctor. Without the earlier edition, the name "Brunot's Island" would be meaningless—a simple landmark, with instructions to find the "channel on the right" as you proceed downriver where you will eventually come upon Hog Island, Dead Man's Island, Big Seweekly Creek—a place where there "used to be an old French fishing basket," a curious reference, indeed, for an ostensibly practical book.

Seventy-three miles downriver is Steubenville. No explanation of the name is given in the 1808 edition, but the 1837 tells us it was named for Fort Steuben, which was built for protection against Indian raids. The fact that the fort, in turn, had been named for Baron Von Steuben, the Prussian general who undertook to train American troops in the Revolutionary War, wasn't mentioned. Which is too bad, because Von Steuben was something of a bargain, as generals go; he undertook his command on a contingency basis, whereby he would receive compensation if, and only if, the American cause was triumphant.[3]

Before reaching Steubenville, the downstream traveler will have come upon Willis's Creek. A curious entry in

---

[3] This magnamity and idealism notwithstanding, he had a hard time collecting what was due him.

1808 reports that there was a spot on a nearby hill "where in winter the snows are observed to smoke as if warmed by an internal fire." The 1837 edition has no precise entry for Willis's Creek, referring only to "Wills' Creek" in passing; nor does it refer to that phantasmal "internal fire" that the previous generation of boatmen had reported seeing on the snowy hillside.

Six miles downriver from Steubenville, two miles beyond Mingo Bottom, there was once a settlement named Charlestown.

> [It] is situated on the left back of the river, contains about 80 dwellings, a court house, pillory*, jail, an academy, an extensive pottery of stone and queen's ware, a boat yard, 8 mercantile stores, and a post office.

A thriving little community, one might suppose; but it is hardly progressive, even by early nineteenth century standards. The asterisk after "pillory" indicates a footnote that reads:

> What a pity that an enlightened people, in an enlightened age, should so far lose sight of the common principles of humanity, as to set before the door, or public seat of justice, such a disgraceful, inhuman, and savage machinery of punishment.

Today's readers might find this pious expression of disapproval somewhat quaint, for the image of the pillory has been cute-ified and sapped of authenticity through countless appearances in film and cartoons and on TV. But it was hardly insignificant in its use as a "savage machinery of punishment." To be locked into a single posture is nothing for a few minutes; but with the passage of time, the discomfort becomes something entirely different. Malefactors could be sentenced for as many hours as needed to produce real agony; and only a century before, criminals in old Virginia sometimes had their ears nailed to the board.[4]

By 1837 Charlestown had been renamed Wellsburgh, and the number of dwellings had increased from eighty to one hundred, with a population of approximately a thousand people. There were also a "courthouse, academy, several stores, a number of taverns, and two or three large warehouses from which large quantities of flour are shipped for New Orleans." The pillory is not mentioned, which might indicate that enlightenment had reached Charlestown with its new name. Then again, its presence might simply have been ignored as unimportant.

Blennerhassett Island is of course featured in the 1808 edition, for that was shortly after the period of the island's glory. It is fully described in typical late-eighteenth century style, with a sentimental dash of early Romanticism:

> Blennerhassett's Island: "On ascending the bank from the landing…we entered at a handsome double-gate, with hewn stone square pilasters, a gravel walk which led us 150 paces to the house, with a meadow on the left, and shrubbery on the right, separated by a low hedge of privy-sally, through which innumerable columbines and other hard flowers displayed themselves to the sun. The house is built of wood and occupies a square of about 54 feet each side, is two stories high and in just proportion; it is connected with two wings, by a semi-circular portico or corridor running from each front corner."

And on and on in a similar vein. This romantic vision is not the personal testimony of an articulate riverboatman;

---

[4] Daniel Defoe, however, once stood in the pillory for an agonizing three days while a frolicsome crowd chanted his own mock-heroic "Hymn to the Pillory" at him.

its source is literary, as the quotation marks indicate—cited anonymously as: "A Tour From Philadephia, Etc. An original work preparing for the press."[5]

The story of Blennerhassett is well-known. A cultured Irishman inspired by his reading of Rousseau, he and his bride came to America in quest of the Eden that lured so many from Europe during and after the French Revolution. Settling on a large island in the Ohio River, he built a great mansion, furnishing it with fine furniture from London and Paris, expensive tapestries, rare oil paintings and splended mirrors. Like his famous contemporary Thomas Jefferson, he envisioned a life of elegance, learning and ease in the midst of a vast wilderness.

After Aaron Burr visited him, Blennerhassett was implicated in Burr's plot to create a new empire in the west, and was forced to flee his island plantation in 1806, barely escaping the envy, wrath, and patriotic cussedness of the Wood County (Virginia) Militia which plundered and pillaged his mansion. Later, fire and decay finished their work, so that the 1837 edition refers merely to the ruins of the once-splendid mansion. A century later, most of even the ruins had vanished; but in the late 1980s it was reconstructed as a tourist attraction, accessible by riverboat from a wharf several miles upriver in Parkersburg, West Virginia.

A reader might suppose that both editions of *The Navigator* had used up their quotas of superlatives by the time they reached Cincinnati, but such is not the case—there's room for more, and in the exuberant spirit and tradition of frontier hyperbole, neither edition is found wanting. This paean to Cincinnati in the 1808 edition is typical:

> The healthiness and salubrity of the climate; the levelness and luxuriance of the soil; the purity and excellence of the waters; add to the blessing attendant

---

[5] Not listed in *The Union Catalogue.*

on the judicious administration of mild and equi-
table laws; the great security in the land titles; all
seem to centre in a favourable point of expectation,
that Cincinnati and the country around it, must one
day become rich and very populous, equal, perhaps,
if not superior to any other place of an interior, in the
United States.[6]

We are meant to understand that here is a city that is
not merely perfect in the way of your average, common,
everyday utopia; it is perfect with a promise of somehow
becoming even greater. The 1837 edition echoes the earlier,
adding a few flourishes of its own, as well as reporting that
the number of dwellings has increased exactly tenfold, to
4000.

In 1828, however—a date fixed solidly between the
two editions of *The Navigator* and *Western Pilot*—Frances
Trollope came to live in this frontier metropolis with the
purpose of opening a bazaar and making her fortune. But as
presented in her famous *Domestic Manners Of The Americans*, her views on the place were radically different from
those presented in the river guides. Although the title tells
us that Mrs. Trollope's interests were more social than natural, her opinions were enough to contaminate any inclina-
tion for the reader to believe in the salubrity of the climate
and the purity of the waters. Consider this sample of her response to her natural surroundings:

> . . . I never found the slightest beauty in the forest
> scenery. Fallen trees in every possible stage of de-
> cay, and congeries of leaves that have been rotting
> since the flood, cover the ground and infect the air.
> The beautiful variety of foliage afforded by ever-
> greens never occurs, and in Tennessee, and that part

---

[6] Almost a century and a half later, and with typical self-assurance, Winston
Churchill called Cincinnati "the most beautiful of America's inland cities."

of Ohio that surrounds Cincinnati, even the sterile
beauty of rocks is wanting.[7]

This is the report of a woman determined to be miser-
able. Not that opportunities were lacking, of course; there
were plenty of uncouth men who talked too loud and too
much, and bragged too much and drank too much whiskey
and chewed tobacco and spat on the floor and kicked their
boots up on the nearest piece of furniture and kept their hats
on in parlours, and women who walked into a stranger's
house uninvited and pried and gossiped and displayed as
much insularity and ignorance as their menfolk—all of this,
plus their habitually referring to the fifty-year-old Mrs.
Trollope as "the English old woman." Being called old was
cruel enough, but the barbarians didn't even have the cour-
tesy and tact to refer to her as a "lady."

Mrs. Trollope's litany of shortcomings is impressive,
to be sure; but it's doubtful if either Cummings or Cramer
would have recognized the place under discussion—or if
they did, find the things she objected to particularly offensive, much less peculiar. Presumably, their gross insensi-
tivity itself would have protected them from seeing things
as she did—things she considered brutish in typically
American ways, which is to say, graceless, vulgar and simply "inferior."

Frances Trollope was, of course, the mother of one of
the great English novelists, a man possessed of rare judgment and clarity of mind, as all who have read his work will
attest. It was Anthony Trollope who wrote perhaps the
sharpest, yet most magnanimous, and balanced judgment
on his mother's bilious and irascible views upon America:

If a thing was ugly in her eyes, it ought to be ugly to
all eyes—and if ugly, it must be bad. What though

---

[7] NY, 1901. P. 59.

people have plenty to eat and clothes to wear, if they put their feet on the tables and do not reverence their betters? The Americans were to her rough, uncouth, and vulgar—and she told them so. Those communistic and social ideas which had been so pretty in a drawing-room were scattered to the winds. Her volumes were very bitter; but they were very clever, and they saved the family from ruin.[8]

The use of the word "communistic" is interesting, but it was appropriate for the time, and quite precise. It is also only fitting that the famous son of "the English old woman" should have understood the matter so well and expressed his gratitude in the fact that his mother had saved his family from financial ruin in a time when debtors' prisons were still the final solution for bankruptcy.

———————

Inscribed on the mussed and tattered front flyleaf of my 1808 edition of *The Navigator*, in the brownish ink and the flourishes of a well-schooled contemporary hand, is the following couplet:

Steal not this book for fear of shame,
For underneath is the owner's name.

Someone named George Reed was probably the culprit who wrote it, for his signature follows, and is then repeated in various places, front and back. These signatures bear witness to much practice of his autograph, at least, if not runaway narcissism. On the front paste-down his name is followed by what appears to be "August the 4 of 1810."

But what, exactly, is the implied threat in his couplet? The conjunction "for" means "because"; but what can *that*

———

[8] *An Autobiography,* NY, 1883. P. 22.

mean in this context? Is it possible that George Reed was a preacher possessed of such spiritual authority that he could cast the darkness of shame upon anyone who didn't return his book? Or was there a more sinister and immediate threat? Or is it possible that George Reed simply couldn't even rise to the level of doggerel in his verse?

I think the last explanation most likely, because enthusiastic and marginally literate settlers and frontiersmen often found themselves without paper, and were thereby forced to practice their penmanship and autographs on the blank end sheets and paste-downs of books, no doubt dreaming of the day when they would be successful politicians or merchants, and their signatures would initiate enterprise of great importance in the land. Furthermore, it's possible that George Reed was himself a riverboatman; the ability to read and make use of a riverboat guide such as this would hardly qualify as higher education.

In contrast, the only handwriting in the 1837 edition is simply, "James M. Sutgen his Book." No date, no threat. And nothing else, except for an inscrutable, faded pencil scrawl, upside down on the back pastedown. This is difficult to make out, but as I interpret it, it reads simply:

> Cows hide
> Hefters hide
> Calfs hide
> Taken to Outcelts
> In Town Dec 9- 1871.

And that's all. What "Outcelts" might be is unclear, although I suppose it could have been the name of the butcher in town; or George Reed's rendition of a more likely name—"Ousley" or "Ostervelt," perhaps; or maybe even "Hartsook." Then again, the word might be "outskirts." And yet, wouldn't that require a reference to "outskirts *of* town" rather than *in* ? Can an *out* skirt be *in* ? Hard to imagine; and yet, anyone who could spell heifer with a "t" had obviously been liberated from the clutches of a niggling orthography. All true; although the fact that prepositions can sometimes prove more volatile and more susceptible to regional variation than other parts of speech might indicate that outskirts could be just about anywhere.

———————

It isn't simply our speech that changes, of course; everything does. This has been the thesis of my essay, and it is wisdom as old as Heraclitus, who lived two and a half millenia ago. Like the other pre-Socratic philosophers, Heraclitus was occupied with finding some enduring reality behind all the world's change—the *Urstoff*, or primary element out of which phenomena are translated. "Wisdom is one thing," he wrote; "to understand the principle of how all things are translated out of one another."

But Heraclitus's search for the basic stuff of reality led him to conclude that it wasn't *stuff* in the material sense at all—it was the principle of energy or change, which he called fire. And yet, he was also obsessed with how things tend toward becoming their own contraries, and evoked the image of water, fire's opposite, to articulate his famous saying that: "We do and do not step into the same river twice, for we are and are not." Time is relentless in its flow, and it can be known only by change. It is also understood, of course, that the flow of a current is itself the very embodiment of change, far more obvious than those inner changes that constitute our lives. Thus it is that there are two reasons we can't step into the same river twice: the second time, we are different, and so is the river.

Obviously, what is true of metaphorical rivers as conceived by an old philosopher is also true of those real rivers he chose as symbols, for they relentlessly move and alter their courses. As with all change, we sense their variances over time and from without, from some vantage point of apparent stability that enables us to witness a contrary movement. Standing on the bank gives one a better perspective of the current than one would have as, say, a sentient bubble adrift among others. And according to a proverb in ancient Greece, a bubble is what a human being is: we wink for an instant in the flow of time, then pop and go out. It seems probable that Heraclitus knew that proverb, and it's pleasant to wonder if it might have been part of the ideational flux out of which his theory of flux emanated.

It's no wonder that living in a world of change we should crave stability of some kind, something to hang our beliefs on with the confidence that they will be the same tomorrow as they are today. Because such stays are rare, and because none is absolute in a phantasmagorical world of winds, shadows and fluctuating seasons, we are forced to settle for continuity instead of real permanence. Nevertheless, we are grateful for every small token—two old books about a river, for example. Or books that contain information about a man who lived two and a half millenia ago, long before books as we know them had been invented, and was dismayed by the fire of time consuming all that he could perceive of the world . . . a man who argued that this *change* was real and abiding, and nothing else.

That ancient statement about change has remained unchanged for all these centuries. Even translated, it is pretty much as Heraclitus formulated it. The thought is still there, and it is still essential to our wisdom. Its natural habitat is a book, as surely as the natural habitat of a catfish is water, and as surely as that of a river is the land bracketing it. Some things can be known only on the page; shift their letters to a screen, and they are subtly altered.

As I am doing now, writing this text, and they will begin to seek the permanence of a page and the stability of print, bound in a book, its abiding vessel. This is what truth is, of course; it's a word, and the natural habitat of a word is

Figure 1: *Glauber's 1670 book on alchemy,* Golden Ass, *dressed elegantly in a modern binding.*

Figure 2: *This copy of Trusler's two volume 1833 edition of Hogarth is typical of the period's decorative bindings.*

Plate 1

Figure 3: *The magnificent two volume "Pawnee Edition" of Washington Irving's* Captain Bonneville's Adventures *(NY, 1898), with and without heavy oilcloth dustjacket.*

Plate 2

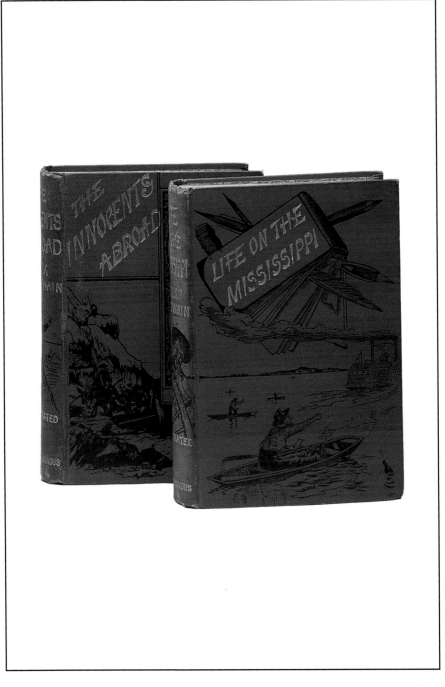

Figure 4: *Mark Twain's English first editions were handsomely
bound in red cloth and are, of course, essential
for any serious Mark Twain collector.*

Plate 3

Figure 5: *Theophilus Noel, sternly gazing out upon an imperfect world.*

Plate 4

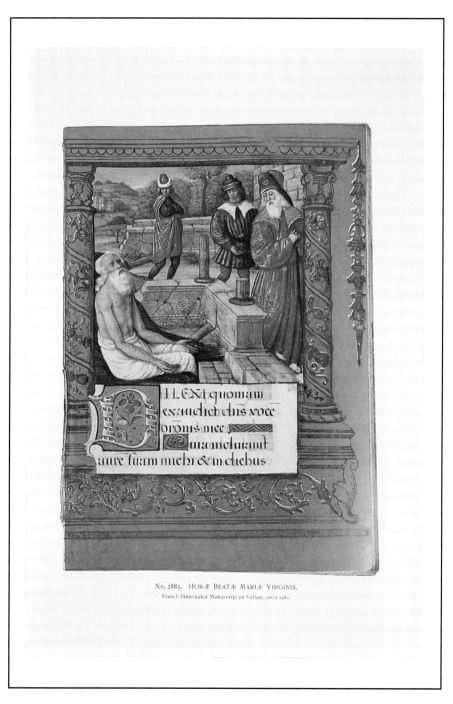

No. 2885. HORÆ BEATÆ MARIÆ VIRGINIS.
French Illuminated Manuscript on Vellum, *circa* 1480.

Figure 6: *Pickering and Chatto's 1902 catalogue features this page
from* Horae Beatae Mariae Virginis,
a French illuminated manuscript, circa 1480.

Plate 5

1375 **COLMAN (George)** The English Merchant, a Comedy, as it is Acted at the Theatre Royal in Drury Lane. 1767. FIRST
EDITION, 8vo, *sewn*   **3s 6d**

1376 **COLMAN (George)** The Fairy Prince, a Masque, as it is Performed at the Theatre Royal in Covent Garden. 1771 FIRST
EDITION, 8vo, *sewn*   **3s 6d**

1377 **COLMAN (George)** and **GARRICK (David)** THE CLANDESTINE MARRIAGE, a Comedy, as it is acted at the Theatre Royal.
1766. FIRST EDITION, 8vo, *half calf neat*   **3s 6d**

1378 —— Another copy, *sewn, wanting the half title*   **10s**

1379 **COLOURED CARICATURES.**—A SERIES OF 79 COLOURED FRENCH CARICATURES *(see reproduction)*, Lettered on
Binding "SCENES DE SOCIETIE," some plates are signed *T. S. Lithl. de Villain,* and others *Lithl. de Delpech* ; they represent domestic and other
incidents in French Life early in the last Century. Folio, *half morocco gilt,* VERY RARE   **£12 12s**

1380 **COLOURED ILLUSTRATIONS.**—HISTORICAL PORTRAITURE OF LEADING EVENTS IN THE LIFE OF ALI PACHA, VIZIER OF
EPIRUS, surnamed the Lion, in a Series of Designs drawn by W. DAVENPORT, and engraved by G. Hunt, with Biographical Sketch 1823. FIRST
EDITION, *with six beautiful coloured engravings,* folio, *original boards, as issued*   **£1 16s**

1381 **COLOURED ILLUSTRATIONS.**—THE ADVENTURES OF A POST CAPTAIN, by a Naval Officer, with characteristic
engravings by Mr. Williams. *J. Johnston, Cheapside,* N.D (c. 1820). FIRST EDITION, *numerous spirited coloured plates* by C. WILLIAMS, 8vo, *calf
extra, fine copy*   **£5 15s**

1382 **COLOURED ILLUSTRATIONS.**—The CUTTER, in Five Lectures upon the Art and Practice of Cutting Friends and
Acquaintances, and Relations. 1808. FIRST EDITION, *with six coloured plates by* ATKINSON *(see reproduction),* sm. 8vo, *half morocco extra,*
UNCUT   **£1 7s 6d**

1383 **COLOURED ILLUSTRATIONS.**—THE TOUR OF DOCTOR PROSODY in search of the Antique and Picturesque through
Scotland, the Hebrides, the Orkney and Shetland Isles. *Matthew Iley,* 1821. FIRST EDITION, 8vo, *twenty humorous coloured plates by* C. WILLIAMS
(see reproduction), old *green morocco gilt, gilt edges,* FINE COPY   **£5 15s**

1384 **COLOURED ILLUSTRATIONS TO THE BIBLE,** a SERIES of 12 FINELY COLOURED VIEWS IN HOLY LAND. N.D.
(circa 1810). 4to, *half russia neat*   **£1 1s**

1385 **COMBE (William,** Author of ' Dr. Syntax,' etc.) The Auction, a Town Eclogue, by the Honourable Mr. ——. 1778.
FIRST EDITION, 4to, *sewn, unbound*   **4s 6d**

1386 **COMENIUS (Johannes Amos)** Latinæ Linguæ Janua Reserata : THE GATE OF THE LATINE TONGUE
UNLOCKED, exhibiting in a natural order the Structure of Things, and of the Latine Tongue (according to the Rules of the Newest Method of Tongues),
with an Etymological Index of the Words, gathered out of the Janual Lexicon, Varro, Scaliger, Isidore, Martinius, and other Classical Autors, and
alphabetically disposed by W. D. 1656. *Engraved portrait of Comenius by T. Cross (see reproduction),* 8vo, *original sheep*   **£2 2s**

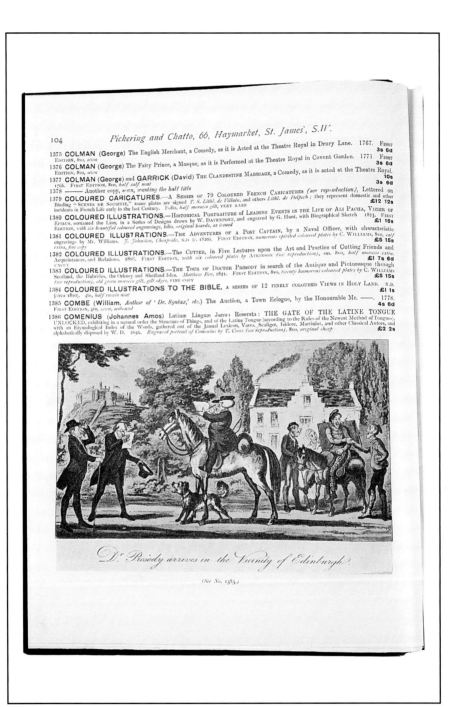

(See No. 1383.)

Figure 7: *Also from the Pickering and Chatto catalogue is this illustration from*
Dr. Prosody in Search of the Antique and Picturesque through Scotland, the
Hebrides, the Orkney and Shetland Isles.

Plate 6

Figure 8: The Consort, *a rare instance of a book issued with two dustjackets (as shown), one within the other.*

Figure 9: *Wendell Minor's dustjacket illustration for the author's novel,* Sassafras.

Plate 7

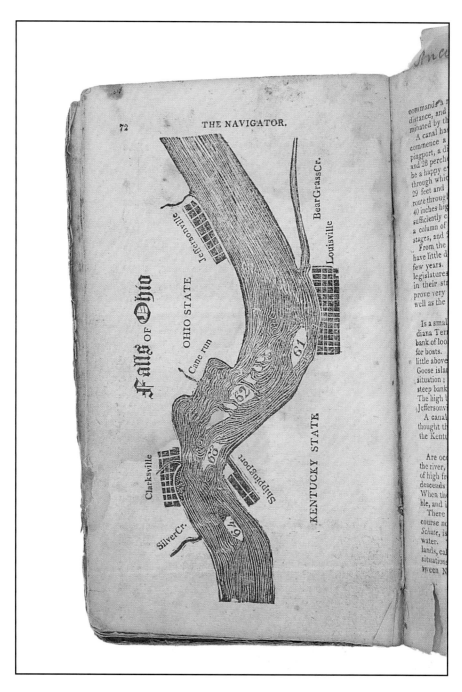

Figure 10: *Woodcut illustration of the "Falls of Ohio"*
(these words printed in quaint Old English type—virtually unknown
for that time and place), from an imperfect copy of the rare 1808 edition
of The Western Pilot, *by Zadock Cramer.*

Plate 8

a book—the older the better. For the years test truths, which come in all varieties and colorations: some can last for millenia, while others wink like bubbles and then disappear. But when caparisoned in print, they suggest permanence, at least, and have a power and dignity like nothing else.

If books disappear, so will most of our history, our heritage, our humanity, as we have known them. And yet, we know that such things will never entirely disappear. The fact that you have been reading this essay provides modest testimony that our old need for reason, continuity and order can still be satisfied in what is very much the same old way.

8

A Woman Great With Child in Pago

In 1974, a Guggenheim Fellowship enabled me to travel to Europe in connection with a proposed novel. My wife, our fourteen year old son and I flew to Norway, where we had some interesting experiences. Pretty much as planned; but not *exactly* as planned, for the Norway I experienced during that brief stay did not fit the Norway of my imagination. Hadn't I read the fiction of O.E. Røllvag and Knute Hamsun? Hadn't I memorized, in Norwegian, the proverb that translates as, "Everything has an end; a sausage has three"? All true; but I was still unprepared.

And yet, our trip was not without profit, and we had some very pleasant experiences. One of the most memorable was traveling on the Oslo to Bergen railroad. Though booby trapped for well-meaning foreigners who did not speak Norwegian and kept trying to occupy the wrong seats, the train was attractive, clean and comfortable. The music of Edvard Grieg was wafted throughout the interiors of the cars, and the snow-capped mountains beyond the windows provided splendid mid-summer panoramas. We stopped for lunch at a mountain lodge, dining on freshly caught lake trout served with carafes of chilled Rhine wine. It was the sort of meal that reconciles disgruntled and inarticulate foreigners to their alienation.

One puzzle remains, however: from the evidence of our brief sojourn, we concluded that there wasn't another fourteen year old in all of Norway. We wondered where their future generations were hidden. Our son wondered, too, although being by nature and vocation taciturn (he *was* a fourteen year old boy, after all), he didn't say much. What he did, though, was catch some trout in several mountain streams, which helped to lighten his spirit—and through his spirit, ours. Once again, the trout god smiled upon us and eased our travail.

Now, all these years later, my novel still remains stubbornly unwritten. I'm afraid it's dead, having expired of inspirational anaemia and chronic neglect at some dark period when the rest of me wasn't around to save it. So I returned from Norway almost as ignorant as I had arrived. Of course we brought pleasant memories back with us; but these memories are somewhat less than apocalyptic; and they did not include anything that would serve as material for a novel. Not even a single chapter.

Nevertheless, I did return with something that has stayed with me, both in fact and in fact's whimsically unreliable ambassador, my memory. While this object alone might not have justified a trip to Norway, I am pleased to own it. I refer to a leather-bound copy of a book printed, not in Norwegian and in Christiania, but in English and in London. It is a small octavo, dated 1631. While anonymous, a penciled note on the front paste-down correctly informs the reader that its author was Thomas Lupton. On the recto of the front fly, another penciled notation correctly states "wormed in margins."

This volume's full and resounding title is:

A thousand
NOTABLE THINGS
of sundrie sorts:
Whereof
Some are wonderfull, some strange,
some pleasant, diuers necessary, a great
sort profitable, and many very
precious.

Directly below the title, is the following poem in the form of an epigraph:

This Booke bewrayes that some had rather hide,
    which who so buyes, their money is not lost:
For many a thing therein if truly tride,
    will gaine much more than twenty such will cost.

And divers else great secrets will detect,
And other more of strange and rare effect.
It is not made to please some one degree,
    no, no, nor yet to bring a gaine to few:
For each thereby, how rich or poore they be,
    may reape much good, and mischiefe great eschew.

The paines and travell hitherto is mine,
The gaine and pleasure henceforth will be thine.

It is evident that already, even before leaving the title page, and in spite of the democratic pleading of this puppy doggerel, we have entered the realm of magic. Its shaky grammar notwithstanding[1], something grand and mysterious speaks out of this verse, something triumphantly implausible. Here is the sort of incantation that promises wisdom or riches or peril…or perhaps some combination of all three. It is the sort of verse that would be found inside a dead man's skull in an old novel.

For *A Thousand Notable Things Of Sundrie Sorts* is a compounded notable thing in itself, a teeming argosy of spectacular human error and superstition. How beguiling such books are for modern readers who can view their preposterous "learning" from the vantage point of a more sophisticated and less superstitious time! The title page alone is enough to show that this is one of those "quaint and curious volumes of forgotten lore" that Poe raved about in his most famous poem.

---

[1] Here and throughout I have left Lupton's solecisms as they are.

And the title page does not lie, for you could search long and hard to find a more extravagant treasure trove of folklore, fact, delirium, credulity, and wild surmise. It is a compendium of antiquated rubbish and golden nonsense. Reading Lupton's book, we are inspired to speculate upon how our own drivel will be similarly admired in some distant future, and for similar reasons. If, that is, the arts of reading and civilization survive.

While I should not leave you panting for a sample from Thomas Lupton's book, and should not tease you further with the promise of having your mind darkened by the shadows cast by such grand and lofty nonsense...even so, before satisfying you in this regard, I will ask you to picture the text, for it is printed in Gothic or Black Letter type. This is late for the period—which is only proper, for my volume is the ninth impression of Lupton's old tome, and it is evidently printed from the original plates first set in 1587.

The type had not been distributed after publication because it was believed that the book would prove to be a sixteenth century equivalent of a modern best seller—a somewhat valid prophecy, perhaps, for in addition to those eight earlier printings, the *National Union Catalogue* lists ten subsequent printings, in one form or other, the last dated 1814. As for Lupton himself—his name was writ in dew. Neither *The Cambridge History Of English Literature* nor *The Cambridge Bibliography Of English Literature* can find a place in their indexes for him. I have always believed that anonymity is possessed of its own subtle and mysterious dignity, so when I learned that there is virtually nothing to be learned about Lupton, I became interested.

The opening chapter, or "The First Booke of Notable Things," begins with an anecdote, one that is longer than most and as near a modern news report as any in the book.

It is a warning against sage, in the form of a cautionary tale about a young man and his true love who were walking in a garden one day, when he idly plucked a few leaves of sage and rubbed them on his teeth and gums.

One can't help but wonder if the young rascal wasn't sweetening his mouth to kiss hers. Lupton doesn't say; but he does say that the poor fellow instantly fell dead.

When the authorities heard of this strange event, they asked the dead man's Love to take them to the garden and show them what had happened. She did, and to demonstrate, took up some leaves of sage and rubbed her teeth and gums with it, whereupon she also fell lifeless to the ground.

Realizing that she had obviously died of a deadly poison, the judge who had witnessed this investigation ordered the sage to be dug up, and it was discovered that under the roots there "was a great Toad found, which infected the same Sage with his venomous breath." Then we are informed that "Anthonius Mizaldus hath written of this marvelous matter," and cautioned that it "may be a warning to such as rashly use to eat raw and unwasht Sage: therefore it is good to plant Rue around about Sage, for Toads by no meanes will come nigh unto Rue, (as it is thought of some.)"

Known to Chaucer, Rabelais and Boccaccio, this Poisonous Toad's Tale is a generic late medieval motif with a dozen versions scattered in as many texts. It is interesting for this as well as for some sixteenth century version of environment pollution, showing how different Lupton's old report of contamination is from the mephitic chemistry that troubles our dreams today. What a grim contrast there is between the noxious toads that poisoned our ancestors' dreams and the wild proliferation of synthetic toxins in the world we know!

The reference to Antonius Mizaldus intrigued me; but my available references revealed nothing. Later, I searched for his spoor in our university library, and learned very little other than that he, like Lupton, lived in the sixteenth century, and that "Mizaldus" was his Latinized name, his native French name being either Mizauld or Michauld. The British Museum lists forty-six of his works, on a broad range of subjects that include meteorology, medicine, celestial harmony, memorabilia, aphorisms, and herbal science.

Not surprisingly Mizaldus is identified as a "miscellaneous writer," and we know by the additional data, or lack thereof, that he was as obscure as he was miscellaneous. But this seems only fitting, for Thomas Lupton was also a miscellaneous writer, and almost as obscure. Furthermore, I am something of an obscure and miscellaneous writer myself, demonstrating once again the secret attraction of like unto like.

I find all this gratifyingly felicitous—partly because we obscure miscellaneous writers should stick together, to be sure, but also because I find a deep and subtle fascination in lives of obscurity. Such lives are, after all, the most "natural," and perhaps—in ways that are not always and entirely clear—the most interesting. Emily Dickinson understood this, although she could hardly be called a miscellaneous writer; even so, she was sufficiently obscure during her lifetime to write a poem with the lines, "I'm nobody, who are you? Are you nobody, too?"

The little parable of the deadly toad that opens Lupton's book is a fair sample of all those 999 entries that follow. But many of the entries are prescriptive rather than anecdotal. This is a book that groans, sighs, and sweats with a burden of fantastic and antiquated nostrums. For example, there is Number 8, on page 3, directly across from the ending of the Poison Toad account. According to this prescription, "Earth Wormes fried with Goose greace, then straind, and a little thereof dropt warme into the deafe or pained eare, doth help the same: you must use it halfe a dozen times at the least. This is true."

That's the complete entry, I'm pleased to report. Also, being partially deaf—what is sometimes sardonically termed "socially deaf"—I am pleased to ignore it. It is only slightly longer than the cure for hiccups, which in various forms lasts on even into this, the Age of Science: "Stop both your eares with your fingers, and the hickop will goe away within a while after. Proved."

Even more laconic than either of these, however, is this sixteenth century version of a sleeping pill: "The soles of the feet anointed with the fat of a Dormouse doth procure sleepe."

———————

Lupton's old book abounds with astrological lore along with other miscellaneous reports of supernatural signs and portents, suggesting that the worlds without and within are governed equally by occult influence. "If a fir tree be touched, withered or burned with Lightning," he says, "it signifies that the Master or Mistresse thereof shall shortly dye." And for those troubled by lycophobia: "If the tayle of a Woolfe be buried or put in the ground of any Towne or Village, no Woolfe will enter in that Town or Village."

There are also liberal doses of oneiromancy. As is often true of such occult messages, these draw upon that primeval power that feeds poetry, even to this day, when we are so enlightened we can hardly stand it. How can one solicit prophecy in dreams? Lupton tells us how, and he tells us in several ways: "He that sleepeth in a sheepes skin, that shal see true dreams, or dream of things that be true." And what sorts of dreams are prophetic? Virtually all, in one way or other. But of course they require formulas for interpreting them, as follows:

> To dreame that Eagles flie over your head, doth betoken evil fortune. To dreame that you see your face in the water signifies long life. To follow Bees, betokens gaine or profit: to be married, signifies that some of your kinfolkes is dead: to dreame that you

worship God, signifies gladnesse: to looke in a glasse, doth pretend [portend] some issue or a childe: to have oyle powred upon you, signifies joy. Michal Scotus and Artemidorus."[2]

But his subject is far from exhausted, for Lupton keeps returning to it, in another place claiming that, "To dreame that you go over a broken bridge, betokens feare: to have your head cut off for a hainous offence, signifies the death of friends: to see hands filthy or foule, doth signifie losse and danger: to feed lambs, signifies griefe or paine." Such dire prognostics are everywhere, for *A Thousand Notable Things* teems with citations of occult correspondences between the dream world and the waking. One more entry will be sufficient to represent all the rest:

> To kill Serpents in your dreame, signifies victory: to see sailes of ships is evill, to dreame that all your teeth are bloudy, it signifies the death of the Dreamer: but that the tooth is drawne out, signifies the death of another: that birds enter into a house, signifies losse: to weepe, betokens ioy: to handle money, signifies anger: to see dead horses signifies a lucky euent of things. Artemidorus.

For one of Lupton's temperament or degree of learning (or degree of ignorance, which is the same quality grabbed by the other end), the whole world shimmers with meaning. Nothing happens without trembling the mysterious web of reality, and with it, oneself. When we enter Lupton's book,

---

[2] Probably Daldianus Artemidorus of Ephesus, who lived in the 2nd century A.D. His *oneirocritica* is, as the title states, a treatise on dream interpretation.

we enter a panpsychistic world of magic, alive with won-drous signification and mystical import. Past and future are so tangled in the present, it is no wonder that prescriptions in time are forthcoming. It is no wonder, too, that we should all come alert when we are stung by such nonsense, for they provide ignorance for us, and we live by ignorance as much as by knowledge, craving both of these great transactionals with equal passion. We always have, and always will. Or, to put the matter more politely, we live by manifold fictions, which we tacitly conspire to believe in as faithfully as if they were stamped in iron. What would we ever do without them?

Wonders exist only at a distance, for with proximity they cease being wonderful. This distance is often conve-niently that of some future time, therefore invulnerable to disproof, for how can events be disproved while they are still only predicted? Such things can no more be criticized or discredited than vaporous plans for a novel with a Nor-wegian locale for the scene in one chapter. It is this way with all prophecies, and Lupton is not hesitant in providing gaudy samples, such as that which follows, referring to mystical phases of the moon and those earthly seismic tremors that have always fascinated and perplexed hu-mankind:

> Many that are borne at that time, when the earth doth quake, are always feareful: in the time of thunder, they are for the most part faint and feare-full: in the time of the change of the Moone, either they live not long, or else they be weake and often-times, as Aristotle saith, have Melancholike dis-eases, or else are out of measure Melancholike: which makes them to be waiward, fretting, and sel-dome merry.

When Lupton wrote his book, much of the world was as remote as the most distant conceivable future. Indeed, other places are a sort of future for us, or used to be, in that they could be known or reported upon in greater detail only over an interval of time; conversely, the future is simply another faraway place, only it is one that will some day surely be visited, if not by us, by others.

While this notion retains some validity today, how much more compellingly true it seemed to Elizabethans, a time when mariners returned to England with their heads filled with wonders—virtually none of which they had actually witnessed, of course; and for that reason as outlandish as rumor, fear, ignorance, boredom, gullibility, and human imagination could make them. And yet, who could gainsay the most extravagant of these reports from afar? Ignorant seamen returning from the ports of Scandinavia, Greece, and Portugal brought back stories that might cast civilization in a trance for centuries, or stagger the sun and moon in their courses.

Thus it is that I now arrive at the woman in my title, who inhabits a short entry on page 80 of Lupton's tome:

> There was a certaine woman great with child in Pago, not farre from Andernacus, a Towne of the Bishop of Cullen, desiring or longing to eat or to feed on her husband's flesh, and although she loved him intirely, she killed him in the night, and being satisfied with the halfe of his flesh, she powdred the rest with Salt, but after when her great longing did cease, and that she did repent the deed, she did confesse it to her friends that sought for her husband.

This edifying account is ascribed to "Iohannes Langius, in his medicinall Epistles"; after which Lupton adds his own prudential caution: "Therefore it is good for the husbands to take heed, while their wives have such inordinate longing in them."

Female cannibalism was evidently a contemporary flourish upon the obsession with sex and violence that still remains with us. Lupton obviously found the subject newsworthy, and elsewhere reports upon a woman who in following a priest wearing sandals, was so excited by the sight of his naked ankles, she threw herself upon them, grabbed them, and started gnawing upon them until the poor fellow somehow managed to rise above the situation and escape.

Most of these singular events were thought to have happened in what were then distant parts of the world, allowing room for the imagination to work its mischief. It's something of a pity that we today are denied the satisfactions provided by all those anecdotes spawned by ignorance and the bedazzled reports from such remote distances; but our TV sets—those nosy spoil sports—bring all the exotic places of the world into our front rooms, showing that, essentially, such regions appear to be filled with people wearing jeans and T shirts as they dance to savage rhythms scarcely less civilized than those on our FM stations.

But one more anecdote about an exotic and magic land needs to be told, for this is one of the early references to the indigenous inhabitants of the New World and their custom of chewing tobacco:

> The Indians doe use the Tobacco (a notable herb), for to indure the growth, and also for to suffer hunger, and to passe dayes without having need either to eat or drinke, by any desart or dispeopled Countrey, where they shal finde neither water nor meat. They doe use of these little balles, which they doe make of this Tobacco, they take the leaves of it, and doe chewe it, and as they goe chewing of them, they mingle with them certaine powder made of the shelles of Cockles burned, and they mingle it in their mouth all together, untill they make it like to Dowe, of he which they make certaine little balles, little greater than Peason [peas]: and they keepe them and use them, for the avoyding of hunger and thirst in their trauell, without any meat and drinke,

for the space of three or foure dayes. This Doctor
Monardus hath written, with many other wonders
and notable vertues thereof, in his Booke before
mentioned, intitled, *Joyfull Newes Out Of The New-
Found World.*[3] This Tobacco is a maruellous and
wonderfull herb, growing in the west Indias, called,
the new Spaine: and thorugh the bringing of the
seedes thereof from thence, it growes now both in
Spaine and France.

In spite of all their fascination, however, Lupton's nostrums
and medicinal charms do not quite match the brief stories
he tells, gathering them in from all times and directions,
with an appetite that is both lusty and eclectic, wild and
shrewdly mercantile. The reader cannot help but respond to
so much, and wants to know what happens when the thirti-
eth entry of his sixth book takes off from a passage in Pliny
the Elder, beginning with the magic words: "A Tode being
strucken of a Spider, or of a Serpent, doth helpe her self by
eating of planten," and continues as follows:

For confirmation whereof, a Tode being on the
ground, hard by a wall, a Spider did suddenly strike
the said Tode on the backe: Which when the Tode
felt, beginning to swell, did eat of Planten nigh unto
the place. Whereof being well, the Spider againe did
poyson the Tode with her venome as before. Which
done, the Tode preserved her self with the said
Planten as before: but one that chanst to behold the
same, did then cut up the said Planten, and tooke it
away from that place. Which Tode the third time be-

---

3 Nicolas Monardes was a Spanish physician, whose *Historia Medicinal de las
Cosas de Nuestras Indias Occidentales* (Seville, 1574) was translated by John
Frampton, part of which was first printed in London in 1577.

ing strucken or rather poysoned of the Spider, as before, immediately searched for the said Planten, for
(as it should seeme) there was no more Planten nigh
to that place, which when shee could not finde, did
swell so sore, that soone after shee did burst withall.
The party that did take away the same Planten, and
did see this strange and maruellous matter, did tell
mee this for a very truth. Whose credit I know to bee
such, that I am bold here to place the same, hauing
such good occasion. And I heard that a Noble man
of this Realme, did see the like.

This story is a good one; and so far as I know, it is not
inherently impossible, although I have little knowledge of
spiders or toads, or how inflatable the latter might be when
swollen from poison. The spelling of "tode" is curious, too;
it's as if Lupton has forgotten that he spelled it differently,
elsewhere. But it is typical of his age to demonstrate a magisterial disdain for those orthographical proprieties that did
not yet exist and spell "toad" two different ways in the
same text. Lupton's use of "strucken" is also worthy of our
admiration; this is obviously far sturdier, libertarian, and
fun-loving than those more familiar domesticated forms,
"struck" or "stricken."

While there is much giddiness and folly in Thomas
Lupton's quaint book, the reader is occasionally jolted by
what appears to be nothing less than sober, evidential fact.
Consider what he has to say about the longevity of different
species:

It is said that a Hare doth liue ten yeares, the age of a
Cat is so much, a Goat doth liue eight yeares, an Asse
thirty yeares, a Sheepe, ten yeares, but the Belweather
many times doth live 15 yeares, a Dog 14, but sometimes 20, a Bull 15, but an Oxe, because hee lacks his
stones, doth liue 20, a Swine and a Peacock 25, a
Horse 20, and oftentimes 30, there have been Horses

that lived 50 yeares. Pigeons live naturally 8 yeares, a
Turtle and a Partrich 25 yeares, and also a kingdove,
which oftentimes liues 40 yeares. Mizaldus.

The "turtle" referred to represents a folk etymology of
the Latin word *turtur,* which is imitative of the cooing of a
dove; but I seem to remember coming upon a reference
years ago to the effect that the "turtle" of "turtle dove" was
a folk assimilation of the old Persian *turtar*, which meant
simply "dove"; but I can't find any supportive citation for
this, so I may have dreamed it… which might have foretold
that I would some day imagine it was not a dream at all, and
maybe even refer to it in an essay.

As for the lifespans cited: they seem entirely plausible,
although today housecats tend to last longer than ten years.
As for horses, I can't remember ever hearing of one that has
lived fifty years. And yet, given the short breeding cycles of
animals, along with the fact that they are bred by humans
for specific traits, it is quite possible that lifespans have
changed. And, while the stated lifespans for dogs seem generally plausible for me (although I have never personally
known of a dog to live twenty years), there is a far greater
time period for gradual genetic change in *canis familiaris*
than in the human species—even if we were as eugenically
concerned with our own progeny as with that of our domestic animals.

I purchased my copy of *A Thousand Notable Things* from a
clerk in an antiquarian bookstore in Oslo, from whom I
later bought a leather-bound London, 1832, copy of James
Fenimore Cooper's *Lionel Lincoln*, with a fore-edge painting of Boston harbor. When I was unable to find anything I
wanted in the stacks of their Oslo store, the clerk told me
that he had some old volumes in his home that I might be
interested in. He described them; I told him I was inter-

ested, and visited him that evening, whereupon he greeted me with two stacks of old and interesting titles.

In my view, the most desirable of these were, of course, the titles referred to above. His price for Lupton's book was the U.S. equivalent of about $140; but when I offered an even hundred, it was accepted. Later, after an exchange of letters, and at the urging of my wife, who has a special fondness for fore-edge paintings, I bought the copy of Cooper's novel. I was happy to pay $100 for it, also. You should not infer from these facts that $100 is the only price I pay for books; I have often paid much less. But for these copies, $100 seemed a good price, and I was happy to get them.

They are still in my collection—Cooper's novel with the fore-edge painting, because it is beautiful, and Lupton's book, because of its antiquarian interest, which is in turn a reminder of our extraordinary human capacity to believe in just about anything, no matter how extravagant—poisonous toads and dreams of earthquake and sleeping potions made from the fat of a dormouse . . . and last, but not least, the cannibalistic impulse of ravenous females, fired by the excitement of seeing a man's naked ankles.

And yet, one might conceivably argue that there is something adventurous, grand and even quirkily heroic in these testimonials to our foolishness, for they represent a triumph of imagination over the quotidian constraints of actuality. Why should we be so utterly confined to some notion of the real if we have the power of invention? What kind of reality is it that keeps betraying us by vanishing relentlessly in time?

Such niceties lead us naturally to the venerable old epistemological/ontological question of what, exactly, anybody can possibly mean by the word "reality." Hard to say. I can remember having a conversation with a physician several years ago, when the subject of fiction came up, and I asked if he like to read novels. "No," he said, "I am a realist."

I confessed that I might be tempted to join the ranks, if I knew where to enlist. Nevertheless, part of me was pleased with his answer, for who would want a physician to be anything *other* than a realist? Of course, philosophically speaking—and no matter how it's defined—what we mean by "reality" can take us only so far in understanding ourselves and the world we are part of. Not only that, we're all realists in one way or another. No doubt Thomas Lupton was a realist to his own way of thinking; and look at some of the things *he* came up with.

9

Dust Jackets and the Art of Memory

*T*he great period of decorative bindings for American trade books began in the 1880s and ended in the 1920s, when cloth bindings as a pictorial medium were generally replaced by the paper of dustjackets. As far back as their introduction in the 1830s, dustjackets had been purely utilitarian, and as devoid of decorative display as sandbags or hip boots. Indeed, the contrast between the dull, featureless dustjacket of books in the 1890s and the lavish arabesque designs they concealed could be startling.

Their minimally functional drabness helps explain why old dust jackets are so scarce. Why would anyone bother to save a sheet of coarse, cheap, plain paper folded to fit a book? Or paper with nothing but the title of a book and the name of its author printed on it? Such wrappers had about as much character as the paper old-time butchers used for wrapping catfish and sausages in. Then along came the jazz age, and the tempting possibilities of the dustjacket as a pictorial and advertising medium could no longer be resisted.

It's easy to scorn first-edition collectors and their fastidious concern over completeness and condition. And when it is reported that some dust-jacketed copy of a first edition has brought ten or twenty times the amount of one without the dj at auction, it does seem to be head-scratching time. But passions and obsessions cannot be truly measured from without, for they are interior phenomena; and if they're generally harmless, they should be accepted as exotic growths—a little like fungi and parasites, perhaps, or those pale blind fish in those other, more spectacular interiors, the dark bowels of caves.

Even so, when one realizes that dust jackets have become an integral part of whatever is meant by "first edition," more than a call for compassion and forgiveness is required; a preoccupation with them suddenly doesn't seem quite so frivolous or *recherché*. Here, as in so many contexts, John Carter's testimony is instructive. Dust jackets, he writes,

> can be of artistic interest; they may have an illustration not in the book itself. They may contain a "blurb" written by the author (admittedly not usually easy to identify), or preliminary comments by critics of distinction. They nowadays normally contain biographical information about the author and often a photograph; sometimes bibliographical details of his other books. How many jackets for Mssrs. Faber and Faber's volumes of poetry had blurbs written by T.S. Eliot, for many years one of the firm's directors?

Since authors are sometimes asked to provide dust jacket blurbs for books other than their own, collectors of the first editions of, say, Sam Pickering or Stephen Jay Gould or Joyce Carol Oates will want to gather in not only all their first trade editions, along with any signed limited editions they may have had published, but all those books for which they have written dust jacket blurbs. The puff that writer X provides for the dust jacket of a book by Y takes a modest but legitimate place among X's first editions, even if it consists of no more than a half-dozen words.

For example, collectors of "Books about Books" will naturally find the works of A. Edward Newton congenial; in which case, they will want to own all his first editions (with djs, of course, and signed or inscribed, when possible). But they will also collect all those books whose dust jackets feature puffs written by him. Even the briefest commentary will be viewed as essential to a collection—as in Newton's nine-word puff for John T. Winterich's *A Primer Of Book Collecting*: "An invaluable little book. It has my unqualified endorsement."

BAB collectors naturally cherish such connections. The collectibility of Winterich's book is enhanced by Newton's comment. But does this mean that one who collects both Newton and Winterich should seek out two copies, one for each collection? I don't even want to think about it. Whatever the issue of *that* issue, however, the bottom line is that gathering these satellite ephemera of an author can provide a special challenge and pleasure.

It seems that no writer can be too famous to write a dust jacket puff. Andre Gide praised the novels of the young George Simenon, and D. H. Lawrence praised Edward Dahlberg's first novel, *Bottom Dogs*. Sigmund Freud gave a puff for Claudia de Lys, quoted on the dj of her *A Treasury of American Superstitions*. "I've spent many fascinating hours with Claudia de Lys," the great man is quoted as testifying, "discussing early religion and symbolism. . . . She seems to have been born with an understanding of these things; a penetration I'd call innate. . . ."

While Freud's generous endorsement speaks well of Claudia de Lys herself, it is somewhat ambiguous relating to the book in question. One can't help but wonder what words were deleted. Still, the general purport is laudatory, and no doubt helped sell copies of the book. And yet, why didn't Freud speak more directly of the specific merits of the book itself? And why didn't the publishers ask him to do so? Or did they think his name alone was sufficient to dazzle potential buyers and lure them from a closer scrutiny of what was actually said . . . and what was left *un* said?

The point here is that whatever interest we might find in those questions derives from the dust jacket rather than the book. Not only does the jacketless book provide no hint of Freud's approval of the author, it tells us nothing about the man's interest in "American" superstitions, as such (although we would surely be tempted to assume it), or his approval of Claudia de Lys's "penetration."

The matter is further complicated by the possibility, at least, that Freud had not even read the book at all (he would not have been the first to be guilty of such an evasion), but simply liked and respected his friend enough to help her out. Then, too, I suppose one might even wonder if the two were not more than just "friends"…but that line of speculation is best not followed, for at this late date there'd be no profit in it—as even Freud himself might agree…even though the question it raises is one a Freudian would surely be tempted to ask.

Existing in time, dust jacket rhetoric is possessed of the idiom of the day. Older puffs and front-flap copy seem sedate by today's standards. Reflecting so much of our time, the tendency has been toward the grim and dire. Consider L. Woiwode's *What I'm Going To Do, I Think*. Informed that the author is "an astonishingly mature artist," we are then told that he

> writes about the large and chaotic emotions of jeal-
> ousy, love, hate, and revenge with a sureness that is
> rare. His story telling is so immediate, it is the expe-
> rience rather than a recreation of it.

While this gaseous testimony lacks certain key terms (e.g., "unforgettable," "stunning," "powerful," "riveting," "inspired," "shattering"), it is unmistakeably the prose of the dust jacket as it had been perfected by 1960 and has pretty much continued to dominate the genre since. Reflective of general cultural shifts, dust jacket prose emphasizes and aggrandizes the darker and more primitive and—as the quoted passage explicitly states—*chaotic* aspects of the human condition.

Pictorial fashions have changed even more tellingly than dj prose. The art-deco jacket designs of the first editions of Faulkner and Hemingway in the twenties and thirties provide a unique and especially meaningful glimpse into the times when the books were designed, published, marketed and purchased by a public whose first acquaintance with the book was naturally, and to some extent mediated by, the dust jacket—a public who understood and responded "naturally" to what the jacket designs communicated in ways which later generations can reconstruct only tentatively and indirectly.

In spite of the old saying, a book sometimes *can* be judged by its cover—or at least its vintage can often be judged within a decade or so. Certainly, this is true of dust jackets. In *A Primer Of Book Collecting*, referred to earlier, John T. Winterich pointed out that the jacket his passed through six evolutionary phases, as follows:

> 1. Plain unlettered wrapper.
> 2. Protective wrapper with name of book and author on face or backstrip or both, in plain type—a simple label .
> 3. Protective wrapper with name of book and author displayed with some attempt at effectiveness—a stage above the mere label—and perhaps with an illustration from the book.
> 4. Same as No. 3, with addition on back of wrapper (hitherto blank) of advertising text, but not about the book encased in the wrapper.
> 5. Wrapper with an approximation of the blurb copy of today, plus an eye-catching layout.
> 6. Same as No. 5, with addition of listing and descriptions of other books on back cover.

Winterich's book, it goes without saying, belongs to the

sixth evolutionary stage; but since its publication in 1935 (the first edition was published in 1926), the dj has entered a seventh and eighth phase, featuring a shift from advertising other titles by the publisher to puffs that promote the book's author exclusively.

Then in the eighth phase, significantly overlapping the seventh, the author's photo began to appear. Only five years after Winterich's second edition, *For Whom The Bell Tolls* was published with the first state of the dj lacking the photographer's name on Hemingway's photo—an important first-issue point for an otherwise common book.

In a way it is surprising that there has not been more experimentation with dust jackets. It is impressive to contemplate how little they have remained unchanged, without significant deviations in either size or conformation. Why hasn't someone designed a perforated dust jacket, for example? Or one shaped like a butterfly? Or one that covered only half a book? Or enclosed it like a paper bag? Or a sort of cardboard box?

The only calculated oddity I know of was pointed out to me recently by the poet, editor and bibliophile, Gerald Costanzo, when he visited our old book-storage building (once a saloon) in Glouster, Ohio, a nearby coal mining town. This is *The Consort*, "a romantic fantasy" by Anthony Heckstall-Smith, published by Grove Press in 1965. When it was published, this novel had not yet appeared in Great Britain; "For the last three years," the dust jacket states, "it has been suppressed on 'legal advice' . . . because of the fear that it might be construed as a lampoon on the royal family."

Suitably, the dust jacket shows the painting of a pale and polite royal couple face-on, dressed in robes. But the dj is in duplicate, one covering another; and the inner jacket is precisely identical to the outer, except for one startling difference: in the place of the queen standing beside the king, or royal consort, there is a naked and spectacularly endowed young woman of dark complexion.

Occasionally one comes upon djs that are duplicated by accident, so that one finds two of them folded together over a single copy; but this is no more than a bindery's wrapping error. The dj of Heckstall-Smith's book is the only example of an intentional doubling I know of. It also demonstrates how much society has changed since it appeared; the prudishness implicit in its publishing history seems almost Victorian by today's standards. Or *lack* of standards, as the case may be.

Even though dust jacket art is a recent phenomenon, there are already masters in the field—artists like Edward Gorey, Maurice Sendak, and Ben Shahn, for example; or Wendell Minor, who is certainly one of the most gifted. Minor's paintings can be found on the dust jackets of a great range of writers, including John Hersey, Mary Higgins Clark, Toni Morrison, Paul Theroux, Judith Rosner, Ray Bradbury and other celebrated literary figures of today. His jackets are not merely "decorative," in the usual, often somewhat pejorative sense, but valid in themselves, even as they open up possibilities for interpretation that gladden and awaken the spirit.

Of course they are derivative in the special sense of being illustrative of the books they are designed to serve; but they rise above such service, even as they perform it. "I build the church," Pat Conroy wrote in a recent book on Minor's dust jacket art, "he makes the stained glass windows."

The promptness with which we adapt to new ways is a constant marvel. Protagoras and Heraclitus were both right—fashion is king, and the fashions keep changing. Combining the testimonies of these two ancient philosophers leads to a wisdom that seems to have a uniquely modern bite: we are so quickly absorbed by the latest custom that the hair styles of a previous generation can look as exotic as those in old photos of the Bakalai or Melanesians.

Thus it happened that James A. Michener reported upon being "startled by the barren look" of one of his novels when he came upon it unclothed, lacking the dj. Notwithstanding their addiction to extravagant design—as manifest in books printed by the Kelmscott Press—most Victorians would have been startled in the other direction upon seeing a modern dust jacket, no doubt finding its embellishments gratuitously bizarre and its self-advertising vulgar.

Wendell Minor is far from being the only gifted dj artist, but he is clearly one of the best in a time when the medium has for several decades been flourishing grandly. Much of his best work synthesizes the values of folk art and realism, with an impact that is not only impressive, judged simply as "free art," but especially effective for its vital purpose in representing, packaging, and marketing the book.

Such a fact should not prejudice any sensible person against his work, of course, for there is no intrinsic reason that a painting has to be devoid of commercial usefulness to succeed as art; and indeed acknowledged classics have been used for the same purpose—the only invidious comparison being that the one seems to have been conceived in and for itself alone, while the other does not.

But in view of the tyranny of trends and styles in free art, such an assumption is a troubled one, for no artifact has ever been as spontaneous and free as we like to suppose. As for the commercial dimension of his work, Minor's dust jacket art has upon occasion proved impressively influential, and it is estimated that one of his jacket paintings increased the sale of a book by 75,000 copies—an astonishing figure, if it is true. Or even if it isn't.

And yet, for all their pictorial elegance, many old-fashioned book lovers find it difficult to think of dust jackets as being in any way condign with the printed text within—for print, as an instrument of interior meanings, is the meat and matter of their passion. A great book, as non-collectors like to argue, transcends its avatars in paper, cloth and leather. If you have read Anthony Trollope's novel, *Dr. Thorne*, they argue, you have read it equally, no matter what copy of what edition you have actually held in your hands.

This sounds sensible, of course; although it's not entirely accurate, for the medium always affects the message, and the different type fonts, page designs and paper of different editions of the "same" book are necessarily to some extent different, no matter how trivial those differences might appear to be. Beatrice Warde's definition of print as a "crystal goblet" is eloquent testimony to an ideal; but in truth, no medium is diaphanous. Furthermore, there have occasionally been radical differences in the different appearances of the same text. Indeed, the history of bibliographical research teems with the evidence of books that have possessed startling variations in the different printings and editions of what is ostensibly the same title.

For centuries books have been idealized almost to the pitch of spiritualization. In spite of their contents, however, they are not ethereal; they are physical artifacts made of cloth, leather, paper and ink. The packaging of a book, therefore, is never utterly extraneous to it or irrelevant. The book itself is a package, and we are obliged only to understand the layers of its translation into form, coming to it from dustjacket, to binding, to printed leaves…and finally to that matter which is not matter at all, but spirit.

The influence of the dust jacket is not entirely confined to the marketing of a book. There is an odd little story about *The Great Gatsby*, concerning the origin of the famous billboard featuring T. J. Eckleburg, showing his faded, bespectacled face brooding over the "valley of ashes." As Nick Carroway, Fizgerald wrote: "Evidently some wild wag of an oculist set [it] there to fatten his practice in the borough of Queens, and then sank himself down into eternal blindness."

According to this story, at some time during the exchange of drafts and galleys between Maxwell Perkins and himself, Fitzgerald chanced upon an artist's preliminary sketch for a dust jacket that for some incomprehensible reason featured a billboard showing the face of an oculist wearing spectacles. This image so inspired and fascinated Fitzgerald that he worked the Eckleburg motif into the novel, weaving in associational images taken from T. S. Eliot's recently published *The Waste Land* in order to create a symbol of spiritual sterility and decay.

It's an interesting story. Unfortunately, I can't remember how I came upon it, nor can I find clear documentation of it. Who knows? Maybe I dreamed it. And yet, it is plausible in a general way, for it is consistent with the tentative and heuristic writing habits of most writers, including Fitzgerald himself. It also expresses something of the dialectic between Fitzgerald and his "editor of genius," Maxwell Perkins, as well as articulating something of the deeper dialectic between visual image and the written word in a novel that is so rich and vivid with cinematic detail.

It is hardly surprising that the art and design of dust jackets should flourish in our time, the age of the image. Not only have modern print technology, computers, television and film exalted pictorial values to an extent unimaginable in older times, they have assimilated them into our basic sense of what reality is. The old philosophical axiom of "To be is to be perceived" has taken on a new and literal meaning beyond that of its first formulation.

The world teems with signals, and the signals keep changing. Why else would we study history and try to learn from it? And to study history in modern texts is often to enter the precincts of a modern period *via* the dust jacket with its unique testimony concerning what has been found there and synthesized into an image of that time and place, while nevertheless leading into the unique world of the text.

Since all things happen in time and therefore come out of the past, it is always interesting to go sniffing for antecedence, a quest that inspires so many scholarly adventures. The seemingly impractical enterprise of seeking the pedigree of ideas may seem trivial in a busy and troubled world, but it is worthwhile, after all. Making connections is making meaning, something we can hardly ever get enough of. Such enterprise is important, it just isn't urgent; and in the world of the moment, urgency dominates the thinking of all but a privileged few, a fact which renders most of our issues political.

There are several obvious influences that have eventuated in the modern dust jacket. It can be traced back through the pictorial covers of the paperbacks and pulp magazines of the 20s and 30s, of course, to the old dime novels that flourished during the second half of the nineteenth century. Also there have been significant European influences, especially out of France and its *livre d'artiste* tradition.

All of this notwithstanding, and with full acknowledgment of its historical and evolutionary development, the modern dust jacket has a distinct style and function. And while its role as a marketing tool does not seriously limit its artistic integrity and achievement, there are, of course, constraints—tacit or overt. There is inevitably some marketing pressure to increase the commercial attractiveness of books; but generally and within certain limits, artists are free to respond artistically to the texts and create as they wish.

And at their best, the results are worthy of our most serious regard. To argue otherwise because they are meant to serve a separate function is untenable; one might as well argue that since a portrait is obviously and to some extent constrained by its subject, no portrait in the history of painting can be considered a work of art.

But dust jackets have another claim upon us, for their artists and designers collaborate in the plenary meaning of a book. An artist's responsiveness to the text is not merely secondary, linear and separate; it becomes an essential part and one aspect of the book's history and physical presence. If contemporary theorists can argue that the reader is an active collaborator in the meaning of a text, can those early readers—the dust jacket artists and designers—be assigned a lesser role? Especially in view of their participation in creating the appearance of the book that other readers will eventually hold in their hands?

I say these things as a writer who is naturally jealous of the text he creates, and yet forced to acknowledge his own very real limitations in creating it, along with his indebtedness to those who have gone before. If the dust jacket artist and designer are given the text to recreate visually, so have I, as an author, inherited rich and vast resources of language, artistic proprieties and literary structures out of which the text is made.

As a writer of short stories I often think of what remains of a story after I have written it and it has been published. Physically, it lasts on unchanged in the book or magazine where it was printed; but what, exactly, becomes of my memory of that story? Somehow, I find this a profoundly mysterious question. I am convinced that it persists in one form or other, but how? Essentially, it seems to me, there is at the heart of a story a still point—an image, a tableau, a gesture that may be said to contain the rest of the story by implication.

This is not entirely unlike a story's opening, in which—after reading it—the entire narrative seems to be implicit. In one sense, it is the opening which is the story's origin, the seed out of which all the events grow. But the central image, the symbol, I am thinking of is buried somewhere within the story; it is to the story's theme what the opening is to its plot. This central image I am thinking of occupies that place in the story where the story becomes most intensely and most unmistakably itself.

I believe this somewhat reflects the function of memory, which is a narrative text as surely as any made-up story. Narrative texts are designed by omitting all but a small part of any event, that small part becoming its synecdoche or envoy. It contains vastly more than itself by implication, thus fulfilling its role as a symbol.

When older people consciously recall their college educations, for example, they evoke images of some very small part that in turn both exemplifies and evokes the whole. The image called forth in one context will not be the image called forth in another, of course; but the remarkable thing is that four years can be represented within a moment by means of a small glimpse of something—a college tower, the campus pond, the walks across the college green, a sorority house, a lecture in anthropology by a young professor with sleepy eyes and a fiery manner . . . each of these, and a thousand others can represent those four years at any one time, according to one's momentary need and the unconscious, individual artistry brought to bear upon the experience.

Similarly, after dust jacket artists have spent hours reading and studying a book, they will go over the notes they have taken along the way (either explicitly or in their memories) and will test them according to their own sense of what the book is—their memory of the book—as that sense intersects with their own artistic values. I do not think that at this stage they are especially bothered by marketing considerations. No doubt such concerns are expressed at intervals in the development of the dust jacket design; but the original impulse is the artist's.

Nevertheless, regardless of how closely they have annotated the text they are to design, dj artists must work essentially with their memory of the text, and their inspiration will be either representational, impressionistic or some combination of the two. Furthermore, their inspiration will draw upon some still configuration, some central image, of the book they have read; and it is from this that the dust jacket art and design emerge.

Something like this was expressed by J. J. Bachofen, when he claimed that "Myth is the exegesis of the symbol." His formula is obviously not to be taken literally, but retrospectively. The famous beginning sentence of Stephen Crane's "The Open Boat" can be seen to lead inevitably into the narrative proper, but only after one has finished reading the story. Thus it is that the story's first sentence, "None of them knew the color of the sky," with its brief symbolic gesture of the survivors clutching the gunwhales of the boat and staring at the ocean—which, as a symbol, embodied their fate...thus it is that all the story's subsequence unfolds out of that first implicative moment.

The central image of a novel or non-fiction text is manifold and highly negotiable, according to time and need. There are as many "centers" and "central images" as there are perspectives into the text; and a dust jacket is an intersection of the artist's and designer's response to what the writer has written. An author will almost surely be surprised by the result, but will understand that what is pictured on the dust jacket is one phase of the book's existence, its journey in time—precisely as every reader's experience of it will be one implication and facet of its plenary meaning.

But unlike the responses of readers, the dust jacket is a static, vivid and specific reflection of the book, merging with it as physical object. Unlike a reader's response, it *stands* for the book to subsequent readers; it becomes part of the book's life, much as an accident or unanticipated journey becomes a part of our lives . . . coming from without, as it were, then being assimilated into our memories, partially redefining what we have been up to that very moment.

Now in closing, and for the sake of balance, it is necessary to cite contrary evidence to all those lyric effusions I have indulged in. It is only right to acknowledge a viewpoint contrary, even contradictory, to my exaltation of the humble dust jacket. Therefore, I will call upon Paul Jordan-Smith, whose *For the Love of Books*, was published in 1934. After arguing convincingly about the arbitrariness and uncertainty of those bibliographical points that torment collectors of first editions, he dismisses dj-olatry in a short paragraph, as follows:

> I ignore, for example, those who make a point of dust jackets—detachable, detestable things that may be slipped off and on at will, and are better tossed into the waste basket. They form no part of the book, and prove nothing.

Subtitled, "The Adventures of an Impecunious Collector," Jordan-Smith's book is everywhere enriched with advice about doing your own thing and not following anyone else's advice. But here the author sounds like a collector who has suffered unfairly in the acquisition of dust jackets, and what is ostensibly no more than personal testimony sounds very much like plain, old-fashioned...well, *advice*. In which case, my advice to you is, don't listen to the advice of a man who gives you advice after he's been telling you not to listen to advice. Especially when he loses all control and over-reacts by calling something as morally inoffensive as a dust jacket "detestable."

But here there is an issue graver than the petulant dismissal of an eccentric writer whose chapter on "Collecting Americans" devotes pages to the work of Elizabeth Maddox Roberts, Robert Nathan, Ellen Glasgow and Louis Bromfield, but refers dismissively to "the pointless pathology manufactured by Mr. William Faulkner"…and doesn't even bother to *mention* Hemingway.

This other issue is not simply one collector's disapproval of the dj in principle, but a new trend in its design. The marketing usurpation of editorial authority and the conversion of trade books into nothing more than product-oriented commodities have had such an extraordinary effect on publishing that one might think of dust jackets as now in the ninth phase of their history.

"Djs," Wendell Minor says, "are designed for people who don't read. Now, it's design for design's sake, and let the contents be damned." He laments the shift to photo, photo montage and other computerized sophistications in today's dust jacket art, along with the waning power of art directors themselves.

As for the artists, they may be asked to bring as many as fifteen treatments for a dj to a marketing committee, who will view the results solely in terms of packaging concepts ("But that's what we're *here* for!" you can hear them cry) and will often reject all fifteen in favor of something they have already tacitly or explicitly decided upon.

Part of this new trend is defended as essential for "down-sizing"; but downsizing, itself, is no more than a trend—which is to say, a phase in the history of the production of books and the marketing thereof. And it is impossible for anyone to predict what the future will be. There aren't any real prophets around, so we'll just have to content ourselves with hope, tempered by whatever historical perspective we can achieve.

And yet, whatever the future brings, up to now the dust jacket has proven to be an essential and interesting part of the history of the modern book. And the historical dimension is our focus, after all; as collectors we love the past, and celebrate it, even as it changes. It's more real to us than newspapers, and even more enduring—its slow and subtle metamorphoses notwithstanding.

Therefore we can rejoice in the opportunities of changing proprieties, even when we disapprove of the latest trends. If we have just come to the end of the golden age of dust jacket art and are entering an age of photo montage and computer art . . . well, perhaps it, too, will generate—and be possessed of—its own idiom, its own genius.

And for those modern collectors who dislike the new decorative styles, there are rich opportunities to appreciate and stock up on all those thousands and thousands of outdated dust jackets that reproduce the paintings of such gifted artists as (to list a handful at random) Leonard Baskin, John Nickle, "Bascove," Judith Kazdym Leeds, Brad Purse and, of course, Wendell Minor.

After all, preserving some version of the excellences of the past—whether that past is one of centuries or decades—is what collectors do. It's what we do, and you might even say that it's what we're for.

10

Inscribed Copies or:
"What the Hell Can I Say?"

*T*he world teems with signals, and we spend our lives translating them. This is nowhere more eloquently manifest than in book collecting, which always has to do with decoding some part of the Past. Specifically, this is manifest in that sort of collecting in which one isolates a particular subject or author that is far distant from the heavy sound of traffic that can be heard in collecting such conventional rarities as the first editions of Dickens or Joyce, or private press editions of Shakespeare.

Many years ago, there was an elderly and very wealthy man, a lonely widower, who had been long retired, his family all grown or dead. This quixotic old fellow spent his days engaged upon a strange quest: he travelled all over the country, staying in motels and hotels of every description, gathering and classifying (i.e., "collecting") the messages other travelers had scrawled in the margins of the Gideon Bibles that such hostelries keep in their rooms.

What sort of messages did he expect to find in such odd places? One can only speculate . . . perhaps, beside the story of Lot and his daughters, somebody's angry scrawl of the single word "Filth." Or in the margin by the story of Noah's drunkenness, "Where'd he get the booze?" Or perhaps, quite independent of the context: a phone number with "For a great time, ask for Marsha." Whether or not the phone number was Marsha's, or whether "she" was any more than a name, is anyone's guess.

All of these, and more; for at the heart of this man's quest was his belief that the Gideon Bibles placed in motels are the modern world's nearest approach to the old family Bible. He believed that one of out great tragedies is the fact that we are a deracinated and homeless population, deprived of those continuities of clan and family that the Romans knew as *pietas,* so that all of the comfortable old symbols of goodness and decency that were celebrated and sentimentalized in 19th century America have been transformed into artifacts that mock them.

I can speak of this man with authority because I made him up. He appears in a short story I wrote, titled "The Gideon Testimony." It is one of those stories whose conception I can remember with particular vividness. While teaching at the Cape Cod Writers' Conference in the late 1960s, I met a woman who mentioned that the familiar Gideon Bibles in hotel rooms often have things written in their margins. I was incredulous, partly because the idea fascinated me from the start and I wanted to believe it too much to believe it.

But she swore it was true, and did so with such conviction that I eventually believed her account . . . which worked out well, in the sense that I was able to develop the idea into a story. Nevertheless, it must be admitted that I have never once—in all my subsequent travels—found a single word written in a Gideon Bible. The nearest thing to a message was a childish ink scrawl, someplace—although I can't remember where. All I know is, it didn't spell "filth," or any other word I could recognize.

———————

My Gideon character was not identified as a book collector, but book collectors will understand him and his passion to record—which is to say, *collect*—marginal notations for the testimony they provide of the human condition. So much sifts out of our lives that we yearn to nail down all that is nailable (letting our metaphors fall where they may), for we yearn to believe that there is nothing that is not potentially interesting; we want to believe that finding anything dull is simply a failure of our understanding or imagination.

While the inscriptions of writers enhance a book in obvious ways, those of some unknown donor are not likely to awaken the spirit. Most are perfunctory, bland and if old enough, a little bit wistful: "To X with Love from Y." There are, however, notable exceptions: one of the most touching and eloquent inscriptions I have ever seen was on the front fly leaf of a small 17th century folio, a translation of Machiavelli: "To my son, Hartley Randolph, in memory of a splendid automobile ride. Sept. 11, 1909." At one time I owned this book, but I regret to say that I either sold it or traded it away—indicative of a depressing lack of judgment, whichever it was.

As with X and Y, however, most inscriptions merely signify that the book is a gift—sometimes dated, sometimes not. A date can often be useful in identifying a first state or issue, if it is earlier than a known second printing; and it always, to some extent, humanizes, warms and particularizes a book. It is pleasant to hold a book that was held by someone who has been dead for a century or two; such connections are humble evidence of both our evanescence and our enduring humanity.

Tokens of ownership are usually names, not inscriptions; but here, too, there are exceptions. Recently I picked up a copy of Leonard Koppett's *A Thinking Man's Guide to Baseball,* NY, 1967, with "George—1967" on the front flyleaf. That's all, except for the familiar smiling face, consisting of a circle, 3 dots for eyes and nose, and a smiling arc. Was George a smiler, and did he do that to identify the book as his? Or was his artwork simply an expression of his high spirits at the moment? I doubt that we'll ever know—a fact one could live with, unlike the fact that recording his name would seem to have no function or usefulness of any sort, unless George was one of a large family of book lovers, and his first name was all that was needed to identify this copy as his private possession.

Other inscriptions are more substantive, shedding light upon the text that follows. My copy of Thomas Stubbs's *Divine Breathings, or A Manual of Practical Contemplations,* is a tiny 32mo, almost a miniature. It was printed in London in 1680, and like so many 17th century theological works, the writing is subtle, grave and eloquent. Stubbs opens his treatise by stating his purpose in writing the book: "As it should be our work to get our Judgments inform'd, so our conversation inform'd . . . ." This statement evokes an epistemological principle with a modern twist: to what extent can there be content without form? Can something like "judgment" or knowledge be said to exist outside of some particular mode of articulation? Stubbs evidently believed not, and so far as I know, most people who've thought seriously about the issue agree with him.

On the front fly leaf, in ink that is pale with age, is an inscription (unfortunately undated) in what start out as apprentice poetic lines, coming dangerously near to being a little verse, with line breaks as follows:

> This little book is very scarce
> it was advertised for in vain
> for several years—it was
> reprinted from this work
> in 1803—by my consent—and
> is still scarce.
>   Saml. Harris[1]

---

[1] "Still" in the last line is no more than a guess; it doesn't look like any other word, however; and "still" seems to fit the context best, in spite of its slight ambiguity.

Most of the most interesting inscriptions are, of course, those of authors. And these are preponderantly modern authors; for, while inscriptions are as old as books themselves (as just demonstrated), the 20th century has been their time of greatest flourishing. In Salvatore J. Iacone's essay, "Inscribed Books and Literary Scholarship,"[2] virtually all the authors' inscriptions cited were modern. The oldest (and it was an impressive one) was Poe's inscription of *The Raven and Other Poems* (1845): "To Miss Elizabeth Barrett Barrett/With the Respects of/ Edgar A. Poe."

John Cowper Powys lived into his nineties, and managed to inscribe copies throughout many of those years. In my copy of his *Visions and Revisions: A Book of Literary Devotions,* a note is tipped in, with:

> John Cowper Powys
> Feb. 11th
> 1915
> "Culture—that is the taste of my Friends—"

But is a tipped-in note an inscription? Maybe, maybe not. Depending. Then is a book's dedication an inscription? Certainly not. Even so, this book's dedication should not be passed over, for it contains its own mystery:

> To Those who love
>   Without understanding;
> To Those who understand
>   Without loving;
>   And to Those
> Who, neither loving or understanding,
>   Are the Cause
>   Why books are written.

---

[2] *A Miscellany for Bibliophiles,* H. George Fletcher (ed) NY (1979), p. 48.

I confess that this struck me as mysterious until the thought came that it must, after all, be a statement of didactic purpose: one writes books to teach love and understanding (although the first two classes of people would seem to remain destitute). If Powys's statement doesn't mean that, I don't know what it means. Although I do know that he is a writer of inimitable and irreplaceable gifts, splendidly collectible insofar as he has not been canonized by the literary establishment . . . in spite of the fact that a few famous literary figures in England have extolled his work.

Of the great multitude of authors who have inscribed books, A. Edward Newton was one of the most generous in dispensing lavish testimony of the moment, which is especially appropriate in view of the fact that he is best-known for his books about book collecting, and his splendid library at Oak Knoll.

Here are some from my own collection—none of them personally inscribed to me, unfortunately, for Newton died in 1940 when I was a relaxed ninth-grade under-achiever at Crestview Junior High School, in Columbus, Ohio, and wouldn't have known the difference between a folio and a mare.

> THE GREATEST BOOK IN THE WORLD, Boston (1925): "I read one of the essays in this book a few days ago and it didn't seem half bad to me—A. Edward Newton, Nov. 1932"

> THIS BOOK COLLECTING GAME, Boston, 1928. "I try never to write a book that will not give pleasure: there is not too much fun in the world. A. Edward Newton, 21 Nov.,1928."

One wonders how much less fun he could have found a year later, after the great stock market crash.

In 1931, Little, Brown brought out Newton's *End Papers: Literary Recreations* in a signed limited edition. The limitation of this edition was a formidable 1351 copies—a ridiculously large number for being designated "limited." At the moment, I can think of only one author who had the *chutzpah* to claim a larger limitation: the irrepressible Frank Harris, some of whose "limited editions" were stated to consist of 2000 copies. But Harris didn't sign those copies; he was no doubt too busy providing salacious material for his infamous autobiography.

Having myself signed 300 copies of a limited edition of one of my books with the Logan Elm Press (now, alas, defunct), I know how slow and tedious signing books can be. I found it a curious experience, and kept trying to domesticate my signature as it galloped and frolicked beneath my hand, almost as if the hand were an alien creature and I a helpless onlooker. Whatever the validity of that notion, I emerged from the ordeal convinced that signing over a thousand copies of anything is a great test of one's capacity to withstand boredom, and verges upon the heroic.

And yet, it appears that Newton not only signed all of those 1351 copies, but actually added a message to some of them; at least he did to my copy, as follows: "Time was when I wanted to be an angel. A. Edward Newton."

———

It is perhaps only natural that inscriptions tend toward the vapid and perfunctory. "What the hell can I say?" was all Charles Bukowski could think to say in one of his books—a sentiment shared by many authors . . . even those who are not famous, for a mere half-dozen inscriptions to friends or acquaintances can challenge the creativity of even the most creative writer.

As for Bukowski, however—his inscriptions were like the man, relaxed, free and sometimes a bit incoherent. In my copy of his *The Days Run Away Like Wild Horses,* he wrote: "To Jack Mathews—Here we go. Another book.

Charles Bukowski, 5-12-72." He mispelled my name, but I doubt if he thought it mattered. Who knows, maybe he'd been mispelling his own name throughout his entire life. His real name might have been McCoy or Yarnell or Lipschitz. How would we ever know? Would it have made a difference? (Actually, I think it would have, although Bukowski—sometimes known as "Hank"—might have disagreed.)

Years ago at a writers' conference a young woman named Sherrie Burns was in my class, and during a cocktail party, she approached with one of my books and asked if I'd mind inscribing it to her. Of course not. "But whatever you do," she said, "don't write 'Best Wishes.'" That struck me as a serious limitation upon my freedom of expression—which, in the signing of books, isn't a whole lot to begin with. But I thought a moment, then was inspired to write: "For Sherrie Burns, with pretty good wishes.'" She accepted the inscription good naturedly, but it was my impression that I thought it was a whole lot funnier than she did, and she may have been right.

There is a special felicity in an inscription fitting the uniqueness of the author, the book and the occasion. A pleasingly subtle example is that of the inscription of Fred Anthoensen in a book whose title page reads:

TYPES AND BOOKMAKING
CONTAINING
NOTES
ON THE BOOKS PRINTED AT
THE SOUTHWORTH-ANTHOENSEN PRESS
By Fred Anthoensen and
A Bibliographical Catalogue
By Ruth A Chapin
With Specimens of its Work, Types, Borders
&c., &c., &c.

PORTLAND, MAINE

THE SOUTHWORTH-ANTHOENSEN PRESS

1943

In the upper right corner of the front fly leaf, there is this simple, tiny, pale and delicate inscription in pencil: "Marshall B. Davidson from Fred Anthoensen. 9/29/48." It seems only proper that a typographer should intrude upon his art with such gossamer tact, signifying his faith in the principle that it is print, after all, which commands and justifies our deeper allegiance.

In a dramatically different context, though also nicely suitable to the occasion, are Edward Dahlberg's inscriptions, which sound exactly as they should: crankily learned, decorous, crochety, solemn. Dahlberg was a wonderful and splendidly unique writer, and I was privileged to share a sustained correspondence with him in the half-dozen or so years before his death. And yet, our correspondence was obviously not *entirely* sustained, for when he sent me a copy of *Prose, Number Seven,* containing a selection from *The Owl of Minerva,*[3] the inscription read:

> For Jack Matthews. Please forgive my poltroon
> silence. Be sure you have my very warm thanks for
> the republication of "The Taylor's Daughter."[4]
> Edward Dahlberg
> Jan. 15, '74.

I can think of no other writer who would so casually force "poltroon" into its adjectival mode.[5] It is, not just a

---

[3] "NY, 1973, p. 31.

[4] A piece I'd included in *Archetypal Themes in the Modern Story,* which I edited for St. Martin's in 1973.

[5] While it's true that the word's adjectival function is not *entirely* unknown, such usage is so rare that it might as well be.

shame, but something of a disaster that Dahlberg's writing
has been virtually forgotten. Not long ago I approached
several publishers about bringing out a small book of our
correspondence, depending upon Dahlberg's renown to val-
idate the enterprise; but none of them was interested; in
fact, one editor declined by pointing out that Dahlberg was
no longer a "name in literary circles." (Knowing this would
have maddened poor Dahlberg beyond his usual, more-or-
less chronic paranoia, vindicating him in his enraged distrust of the world as he found it . . . and little wonder.)

The first paragraph in the selection from *The Owl of
Minerva* will bear witness to the quality of Dahlberg's
prose, an unmistakeable complexion of mind that is manifest in everything he wrote—his essays, his fiction, his letters and, of course, his inscriptions—showing, even in this
brief sample, why he should be read . . . and, because of
that, collected:

> I regret everything I have done. Yet I have small
> hopes, which are as near to knowledge as I can get.
> As the Pleiades set, I gain strength. But for what? I
> do not covet youth. At thirty I expected much. What
> a simpleton I was to chant to Apollo, though I knew
> I was songless as the fishes. Where are those chil-
> dren of my pelting imagination? For years I thought
> of being a writer, some kind of outcast motley. But
> I became a buffoon before ever having composed a
> book. Where was the flamy fennel stalk that I might
> use as a quill? Fitted with ruby vagaries and
> canorous moods, why is it I could never invent one
> conceit? A burden of Sidon to myself, I vaguely con-
> cluded that I could never be an author. I lacked pas-
> sionate animal faith.

The only other essayist I can think of with as vivid and
interesting a signature of mind as Dahlberg's is Sam Pickering, very much alive and . . . well, not *kicking* , exactly, but

writing prose that does what poetry is supposed to do, though seldom does: reflect a way for taking in things, experiencing them—which is to say, thinking and feeling about them. What distinguishes Pickering's special gift is an elfin, whimsical pleasure in all the nooks and crannies in those small proportions of the human adventure that are so easily ignored, but nevertheless constitute what we most of the time *are*. Indeed, in his best essays, Pickering creates a sense of things that is so winsome and telling that it becomes "philosophical" in the deep, old, informal sense of that word.

He tells a story about the fellow who asked him to inscribe one of his books "To Jane," then asked him to add: "ain't love grand?" This was so sappy that Pickering briefly debated whether or not to accommodate the fellow, especially in view of the fact that a sale of the book represented only sixty cents in royalties. But then, reminding himself that sixty cents are sixty cents, he relented and signed away.

Like Dahlberg, Sam Pickering's spirit animates all that he writes, so that his letters and essays are all of a cloth. To convey some feel for his prose, I will quote an anecdote he shared with me by letter, as follows:

> I have signed shirts, napkins, Bibles, but the worst thing I ever signed was a picture. I was in Missouri. I had given two public lectures, eaten two meals (breakfast at seven being one of them) with faculty members, and attended two classes. At six-thirty I had a book signing and was exhausted, too exhausted to think. A woman approached the table with a picture in her hand. I had seen the woman at both lectures. The picture was of her baby girl. The girl was naked and rolled up on her back so her private parts seemed swollen, leaping off the picture. "Please sign this," the woman said. I hesitated, but the line behind the woman was long, and I didn't quite know how to say that signing the picture

seemed odd. After pausing a moment, I shrugged, assuming that the birth of the child was so thrilling that the woman saw nothing odd in waving the snapshot about. I signed, but I had to write around the edge of the photograph, forming a kind of rainbow. Otherwise, letters would have touched the child's privates.

Well, this is almost too good to be true, and if something is too good to be true, it might not be true at all. Not that I would ever accuse Sam Pickering of lying; but I wouldn't accuse him of having a dull mind, either; he is not possessed of a sensibility that is needlessly trammeled by facts. Nor would I accuse him of being overburdened with sobriety.

Indeed, there are benign sorts of forgery, occupying the palest end of the spectrum of white lies, and this is the natural environment of Pickering's happy effusions. In his essay, "The Books I Left Behind," he explains how he enjoys getting rid of his books: "Jettisoning gift books," he wrote, "is particularly satisfying."

To book collectors, there is something in this that is profoundly heretical, but there's also something in it that is not entirely displeasing to the mind. Devils, after all, have a special interest for angels, and at certain stages of the moon, all of us have contemplated commiting dark crimes. Similarly, there is something in the idea of shedding all our possessions that is not only liberating, but not entirely unlike the very passion that drove us to collect them.

But none of this can adequately account for Sam's habit of supplying information that he found missing. "In the past," he wrote, "I never bought a book without inscribing it." Thus, in his copy of *In Our Time,* he had Hemingway write: "Always throw hardballs, Sam." And he had Wallace Stevens write: "My everlasting thanks to the man who corrected so many of my poems in manuscript." And most outrageous of all:

Poignantly, Percy Shelley wrote, "To Sam who has spent many hours trying to teach me to swim—affectionately, Shells." When I showed this to the brightest graduate student I knew at Princeton, she exclaimed, "My God, Sam, you knew Shelley! Why haven't you said anything before now?" "Modesty," I answered . . . .

Come on, now! Did that really happen that way? I feel a little bit like that student, although I'm better informed about Shelley's dates. I also remember the old paradox, once beloved of logicians: "Simonides, the Cretan, says that all Cretans are liars"; and if Sam Pickering regales readers with tales of putting others on, how can they be sure that he isn't putting *them* on, too?

Of course, it doesn't really matter. A Sam Pickering essay is half-story, which is a game that a writer plays, allowing the reader to play it afterwards; this is one way in which a book is always about the past, and book collecting is about *that*. And Pickering's happy and harmless duplicity in signing the names of Hemingway and Wallace Stevens in books is not entirely unlike those seemingly "honest" inscriptions that can impressively inflate a book's price on the rare book market.

For the person who inscribes a book is never the one who wrote it. To write a book is to enter a tunnel, like that which penetrates a great mountain, allowing for the passage of cars and trucks upon some Interstate highway. Writing a story or essay is to dwell temporarily in a different place, shut off from society and the world we share with others; and we ourselves are different when we are there, so that when we emerge, we "go back" to being someone else, our memories already making up stories about what it was like within that deep cloister, where we were engaged in making up some version of reality with words.

And yet, in another way, this testimony remains part of

it. We remain ourselves, after all, even in our most radical transformations. And it is nicely appropriate to inscribe a book, whoever we are, for others, whoever they are. Its part of our testimony, after all. It says we have been here, conventionally citing a particular time and place. We don't have to do it in some ghostly Gideon Bible that does not exist, except in one woman's imagination or, inspired by that, a fictitious short story. It all means the same thing, essentially: "Hello, there; I am here, and you are there. Beyond that, what the hell can I say?"

11

Bookish Lunacies

hile the primary booking adventures lie in the discovery and purchase of old and rare books, in which the promise of reading and possession is intricately implicit, there is another kind waiting to compensate weary and defeated collectors even after they have searched for rarities in vain. I speak of people—collectors, bibliophiles, dealers, scouts and all that heterogeneous class of compulsives who for some reason or other cannot resist buying and accumulating books; but I also speak of those miscellaneous non-bookish fauna whom one cannot help encountering while engaged in the Great Pursuit.

Booking is only one of the many activities that bring us in touch with other people, of course. People are pretty much everywhere. They are an alarmingly renewable resource; and it is our abiding challenge to try to understand and get along with them—which is to say, ourselves. And the best way to accomplish both of these things is to have an excuse for meeting them. Booking provides such an excuse, and viewed properly, the people one encounters are as interesting as any of the specimens you could hope to find anywhere.

But some bibliophiles won't settle for mere interest. Their sights are set higher than that; they want peculiarity. Do bookishness and peculiarity go together? There is evidence of it, reinforced by a venerable stereotype. It is part of our folklore that people who immerse themselves in antiquarian matters—books, especially—tend to be eccentric. Maybe the interiority of the bookish mind isolates us from the conventions and proprieties of the outside world, for books are instruments of inwardness, the home of our deepest passions. Print is essentially and naturally the medium of talking to oneself; and talking to oneself is one of the oldest and most comfortable symptoms of eccentricity. You do it, and so do I; or so I keep telling myself.

It's hardly surprising, therefore, that in my decades of booking I have accumulated not only a great many books, but a number of anecdotes about people who are interesting and, well, *peculiar.* As mentioned, some of those people have little or nothing to do with books as such; but it was in booking that I encountered them. Others among them, however, suffer from an obsession with old books that is as virulent as any infatuation known to alchemy or medical science. People belonging to this second class are my subject in the piece that follows—along with the promise of old books that brought me to them.

I have encountered bookish eccentrics everywhere, and in wild variety. I remember a mumbling, thick-set old bachelor named Roger who lived alone in a small western Ohio city. He had stuffed every room of his small frame house with volumes of every sort. The halls were so nearly infarcted that we were forced to squirm our way between towers of books threatening to collapse in an avalanche from the merest whisper of a sneeze. Roger had bookshelves in his living room, dining room, kitchen and lining his stairway, converting it into a crooked and ascending aisle.

While the books were forgivable, he also kept cats, and evidently never cleaned up after them or let them out. Like that profoundly disgruntled philosopher, Schopenhauer, I am a dog person; but I like cats well enough, and have even owned a few; but for all their worth and charm, cats are neither dogs nor books. Even so, they should be

taken care of properly. The last time I visited Roger, however, the miasma of cat odor in his house was so dense you
could have floated a derby hat on the air.

No doubt my problem was to some extent psychologi-
cal, because *Roger* didn't seem to have any trouble breath-
ing, although he did do a lot of nervous humming. He also
tittered when he laughed, which seemed incongruous for
such a big, beefy fellow. It occurred to me that his brain
might have been affected by dwelling in so pungent and
feral an atmosphere. But whatever the cause, he eventually
became impossible to deal with, turning into that particularly abhorrent sort who can't make up their minds whether
to sell or not—or if they *can* make up their minds, not
knowing what price to ask, living in chronic fear of being
cheated. Roger did all this humming and tittering as he suffered.

It is an old medical axiom that there are no isolated
cases, and this is certainly true of Roger. The terrible anxiety he experienced when faced with the thought of relin-
quishing any of his treasures is far from unique. Holbrook
Jackson is informative here, as in so many bookish matters:

> How many bookmen have wished a favourite book
> to go with them into oblivion I have no means of
> knowing, but that there are many, I have no doubt:
> among them, certainly, is Sir Thomas Browne, who
> expressed such a wish in his will: *On my coffin when
> in the grave I desire may be deposited in its leather
> case or coffin my Elzevir's Horace, "Comes Viae Vi-
> taeque dulcis et utilis', worn out with and by me.*[1]

The fey and ghost-bitten types are another familiar
sort. I remember a house in a small West Virginia city

---

[1] *The Anatomy of Bibliomania,* NY (1950), p. 537

where it was said an old woman lived, and she owned a lot
of books she would be willing to sell. When I knocked on
her front door, there was no answer, so I went around to the
kitchen door to knock. Suddenly, after sustained pounding,
I saw the the brief pale surfacing of her face in the darkness
of the grimy window, as quick and elusive as the flashing of
a catfish's belly in muddy water. The poor creature was ter-
rified, of course; and no doubt mad in every clinical sense
but the application of the label "mad".

Shyness and a distrust bred of loneliness are among
the more common and orthodox symptoms of bibliomania,
along with an addiction to strong drink. In the mid-1960s
there was a dealer in a Boston suburb who suffered from
the passionate delusion that the three greatest American
writers were all women. This was a comfortably eccentric
opinion so many years before the main thrust of the Femi-
nist Revolution.

He was a merry-faced little fellow, with gray hair and
a mad leer on his face. I later heard that he periodically re-
lieved himself of the burden of his literary heterodoxy by
closing his shop and dedicating himself to earnest and soli-
tary drinking for a week or two. His nominations for America's three greatest writers? Willa Cather, Edith Wharton
and Ellen Glasgow—fine writers all, but hardly the "greatest"—a silly label at best, for it is based upon a linear measure that is irrelevant to works of art, which being individual, tend not to be linear but, well, deviant and sometimes
eccentric .

In 1970 while I was Writer in Residence at Wichita
State University, I met Ben Thomas, a pleasant, sophisticated, well-groomed graduate of an Ivy League school who
had collected actively for many years. Shortly after we met
and identified ourselves as fellow-collectors, Ben casually
and cheerfully mentioned that he suffered from "manic-de-
pressive psychosis." Then he told me that in a manic phase
one afternoon several years before, he had gotten drunk,

then entered an antiquarian bookshop in Kansas City where he bought $10,000 worth of books.[2]

Since he was confiding it so light-heartedly to a comparative stranger, I thought it probable that Ben was in a manic phase at the time. Obviously, there is no opprobrium to such a confession; indeed, I thought of it, and still think of it, as *interesting*—in more than the clinical sense of the word. Not only that, it was profitible in terms of my own collecting, for when I showed him a duplicate first-edition copy of Faulkner's *Go Down Moses,* with a fine dust jacket, he was immediately taken with it, saying he had to have it. So I traded it to him for a 1521 copy of the Greek Anthology, printed by Aldus Manutius, along with two or three other books whose titles I have forgotten. And, it should be pointed out, neither of us had been drinking at the time.

I can't help wondering what purchasing value Ben's $10,000 fling would have today after decades of inflation. $50,000? $100,000? Something in that range, I would suppose. As with all such translations, however, it would depend upon a specific transaction—such as the comparative value toward a purchase of a sports car or a home—rather than some scale based upon abstract value, because different things obviously appreciate at different rates. I'm aware that many economists argue otherwise, because they depend upon such abstract fictions as "purchasing power" for their professional standing; but that's all right—they're only economists, after all, and should be tolerated.

One of my favorite book-benighted people was a friend for many years, an eccentric in the grand manner, named Paul Wilkes. Descended from generations of wacky English squires and their loopy wives, Paul was a man with style. Although he was unquestionably, unmistakeably odd,

---

2 This may have been Glenn's Book Shop, a handsome establishment I would soon visit.

it would not, upon first acquaintance, be easy to say precisely *how* he was odd. He talked too loud, but then a lot of people do, which hardly qualifies them as odd; most loud talkers are quite normal; they're just loud. And yet, there are odd ways of talking too loud; and that's how Paul Wilkes managed to do it.

Most eccentrics don't really get out there and do stupendously crazy things: they simply radiate their peculiarities in the little things they do, the way musical instruments sound different from one another in playing the same notes. Eccentricity is more a matter of harmonics—overtones and nuance—than of fact. We know it when people don't laugh at exactly the right time or in the right place, or laugh too often, or stand too close, or too far away, or open their eyes too wide. Or maybe talk too loud in a certain way, as Paul did in his gruff, unmodulated voice that sometimes squeaked, like an adolescent boy's first tentations into the baritone range.

Or perhaps wear their clothes a little differently. This is how I once witnessed good old Paul Wilkes' giftedness as an eccentric. One cold, blustery day I travelled to a farm auction, and was confronted by the unwelcome sight of Paul being there ahead of me, already shuffling through boxes of books. I joined in, of course; but then a few minutes later, when a cold rain started to fall, I put on a rain jacket, and happened to look up in time to see Paul also putting on a coat, only he was putting on his brown corduroy sport coat over his full-length tan *raincoat*. I probably should have tipped him off, but I was too fascinated by the sight to interfere.

Just as Spinoza's Dutch neighbors referred to the great pantheistic philosopher as *Gott-betrunken* -"Drunk-with-God"; so might the folks I am speaking of be called *Book-betrunken.* But it would be hard to nicely distinguish the degree to which their madness stems from their obsession and to what extent their madness is the cause of their collecting. It's a chicken and egg puzzle; but whatever the origin, there's no doubt but what the two qualities exacerbate each other: the madness driving them to collect, and the collecting driving them mad. Fred Sickles, M.D., was such a man—a shaky, frail little elderly retired physician, who seemed to have given up any pretense of being suited to this world.

Many years ago my wife and I bought an old, one-storey building in a nearby coal-mining town. This old structure had at various times served as a barber shop, dwelling, post office and saloon. We filled it with bookshelves that hold something like 12,000 books, which we sold to visiting dealers as well as to the public at special sales. Dr. Sickles drove eighty miles to attend one of these special sales, whereupon he introduced himself, then got to work gathering in books. An hour later, I heard him all alone in a back room, talking volubly to himself as he dug through the boxes on the floor. His monologue was loud, dramatic and uninhibited.

After he had filled several boxes, I helped him carry them to the front of the store, where we stood and chatted for a while. "You know," he said, shaking his head, "when I got out of bed this morning, I suddenly felt so sick I almost passed out, and the first thing I thought was: 'Oh, no! I'm going to miss that sale!'" Most mere mortals of his age would have wondered if they were dying; most physicians would have shifted into a diagnostic mode; but here was a man whose first thought was of the booking opportunity that might be denied him—incapacity or death be damned.

Several years later, I visited Dr. Sickles's house, and found it filled with books, of course, along with hundreds of prints, paintings, small statuary, and other *objects'd'art*, some of them first-rate. He collected widely, with special interests in the Modernists of art and literature—in fact, he had bought an unsigned European painting from me, thinking it might have been an early study by Cezanne. I doubt if it was, but why hadn't the possibility occurred to me? Ignorance and a lack of imagination, I suppose—worse than mere eccentricity any old day.

Sickles told me a story about when he was a young intern at The Johns Hopkins University hospital in the 1940s. He had been assigned to the physician who was treating H.L. Mencken, a patient in the coronary ward, and of course visited the cynical old newspaperman as part of the cardiologist's entourage in his daily rounds. "Mencken was a fascinating man," he told me, "and a fabulous talker. I only wish I could remember what he said."

"But he was already famous," I said. "Why didn't you keep a journal or take notes?"

Sickles had no answer to that, and simply shook his head regretfully. Indeed, the sins of omission haunt all of us forever, and not even the clothing of eccentricity can entirely protect us from the pangs of regret and chagrin.

One of the strangest episodes in all my years and hundreds of thousands of miles of booking, however, occurred in the late 1960's in a picturesque little town deep in the Blue Ridge mountains. On the main street near the town's edge stood a large, handsome white frame house, and the familiar "Antiques" sign in front.

I parked my car next to a gray riverstone retaining wall opposite and went in. The woman who greeted me was a pleasant and well-groomed woman in her sixties, and she was responsive to my inquiry about books, for she herself was something of a bibliophile—which is to say, a dealer and collector, as well as a mighty reader.

"Make yourself at home," she said expansively, opening her arms wide and smiling. "This place is filled with books."

And indeed it was. She invited me to look all I wanted,

and since there were no other customers, she accompanied me as I went from room to room, accumulating a growing pile. She asked if conversation bothered me at such times, and I assured her that it did not. Like most collectors, I've learned to listen and talk as I browse. She was obviously an intelligent and thoughtful woman—far more knowledge-able about books than the majority of antique dealers. Fur-thermore, she was *interested.*

"There are a lot of books upstairs, too," she said. "When you get through down here, you can go on up."

"Fine," I said.

"But there's one room up there I never let anybody go in."

I didn't respond to this for a moment, but when she re-mained silent, I turned to her and said, "What do you mean?"

She laughed a little. "Oh, it's too *cluttered* ! I just don't let people go in there. Honestly, it's such a mess! You can hardly turn around."

I said I understood, and turned back to the bookcase.

"I mean, I would, only it's such an awful mess."

"Sure," I told her.

For a moment we were silent as I squatted and scruti-nized the spines of books and she stood behind me, waiting. Then she said, "God knows what you'd find in that room."

Once again I assured her that I understood.

"But it's just too jammed full of things. You know."

"I understand how you feel," I said for what seemed the fifth or sixth time.

She fell silent again; but her odd persistence got me to thinking for a moment. Nevertheless, I eventually dismissed her fretting as an old-fashioned woman's typical preoccupa-tion with her housekeeping, and her sensitivity about it. I re-membered Freud's notion that women view their houses as extensions of their own bodies, converting simple house-keeping into behavior that is intimately symbolic.

But after another few minutes' silence, she said in a rather distant and forlorn voice: "There's a sign on the door that says, 'No Admittance'."

By now, the light bulb was not only *on* , it was shining brightly. So I stood up and looked at her and waited.

She smiled and shrugged her shoulders. "All right. I'll tell you what: if you want to go in, just go ahead. The door isn't locked. It's the only room up there with the door still on it, as a matter of fact. Don't pay any attention to the 'No Admittance' sign. Just go on in."

"Okay," I told her. "Thanks."

So I went upstairs, deciding to go through the open rooms first, but doing so with my mind bolstered by hope. My hostess hadn't come up with me, so I took my time going through the three rooms, accumulating another few books to add to the stack of fifteen or twenty I had already gathered. Then, finally satisfied that I'd covered the territory thoroughly, I approached the mysterious door that did, in truth, have a sign stating 'No Admittance' nailed upon it.

But when I opened this door, instead of coming upon a jungle of old chairs, picture frames, dusty cushions, cuspidors, toys, garden rakes, boxes of clothing and towering stacks of musty old books—all of those things I had been led to expect . . . there was *nothing*. Not a single thing. Not even a rusty paper clip on the floor. Not even curtains on the window, or—for that matter—blinds.

When I went downstairs with my fresh stack of books, she said, "Well, what did I tell you?"

"It certainly is," I said.

She laughed and began to total my books.

And while she was doing so, I attended to the business very closely and found that she organized the books competently, and then added their prices up swiftly and without error . . . along with a judicious discount in what was altogether an interesting and satisfactory transaction.

Several years later I had occasion to pass through this

town again, and when I stopped, the woman remembered me and greeted me pleasantly. But when I asked if she still had books upstairs, she said no, there was nothing up there now. My wife and I were on our way to Charlottesville, Virginia, and I asked her how far it was.

She paused a moment, and then said: "Sixty-three miles." She not only said this; she said it emphatically, conclusively.

But the distance was so radically off, so obviously wrong, (I knew it had to be well over 100 miles) that for a moment I thought I hadn't heard correctly. So, after looking at some more books for a while, I said, "How far did you say it was to Charlottesville?"

"Sixty-three miles," she said.

I turned and gazed at her, and she smiled. Remembering the empty room, I was ready to believe that she wasn't wired quite right. If she had waffled a little—saying something like "Oh, about sixty miles"—I wouldn't have been so impressed. But the way she said "sixty-three" was so definite that she might have been prepared to add the exact number of yards and feet. So the distance was as obvious to her, and as obviously wrong, as remembering a room as cluttered, and imagining that I had insisted upon entering it, when I hadn't said a word to that effect.

And that was all. Except for the very last time we travelled through that little town, when we sought out the location of the house and found that it had been torn down. Erased completely from the landscape. The thick grass that grew over the ground where that house had once stood seemed to have been growing there forever. All things pass away, even our eccentricities and delusions.

Upon leaving town, we stopped at a small produce stand and bought a few small sacks of fresh vegetables, after which I asked the girl who was waiting upon us if she knew this woman, mentioning her name, and if so, could she tell us what had happened to her.

"No, the girl said. "I don't. But I live out in the country, so I don't know many people in town."

To me, this odd little story is more than a mere curiosity; there is a deep sadness in it.

So far, my humble sampling has not approached the
grandiose lunacies of the bibliophage who parboils duodec-
imos and eats them with a glutinous sauce or the delusional
collector who crawls out from among his books with the
guilty conviction that it is in doing *this* that he is an es-
capist. It does not reach to that pitch of frenzy expressed by
Austin Dobson in his doggerel quatrain:

> Books, books again, and books once more!
> These are our theme, which some miscall
> Mere madness, setting little store
> On copies either short or tall.

And it does not reach the heights of bibliomania as
scaled by some of those great obsessives of the Past, men
such as H.H. Bancroft, Sir Thomas Phillipps and William
Gladstone. None of my examples reaches the empyrean infatuation of the 17th century collector, Antonio Magliabec-
chi, who

> lived in a cavern of books, slept on them, wallowed
> in them; they were his bed and board, his only furni-
> ture, his chiefest need. For sleep he spread an old
> rug over a heap of them and so composed himself;
> or he would cast himself, fully clothed, among the
> books which covered his couch.[3]

---

[3] Jackson, Holbrook. *The Anatomy of Bibliomania,* NY (1950), p. 133

Or perhaps our very own contemporary, a fellow who was said to have gleaned a three-million dollar collection of Americana from institutional libraries—gleaning it unofficially and without cost, as it happened. Not to mention accumulating 50,000 door knobs from old Victorian houses awaiting demolition—perhaps to salvage some small part of their elegance. Like many of those who suffer from manias and delusions, this fellow behaved logically; it's just that his behavior was based upon questionable premises. For example, why would he cut out the eyes at the top of the pyramids on dollar bills? The answer is perfectly reasonable: so they would stop staring at him.

The pathology manifest in the extremes of bibliomania is an old one, although not much older than the smug self-righteousness that inveighs against it. The syndrome was diagnosed by the ancients and has been elaborated upon variously throughout the subsequent centuries. As with certain more conventional neuroses, it seems to be the afflicted who understand it best. In his *Anatomy of Bibliomania,* Holbrook Jackson refers to those poor infatuated bibliomanes who

> buy whatever comes in their way: buy their books at so much a yard. D'Israeli argues a craving only for possession to be the main symptom of the disease, and that weak minds are mostly susceptible to it; their motley libraries are mad-houses of the human mind, tombs of books . . . ; out of Bruyére, he recalls a visit to such a collector, where that   philosopher was like to faint on the staircase from the   strong smell of morocco leather; and out of Lucian, an invective against an ignorant bibliomane who, after turning over the pages of an old book, admired the date.

Reading this in a trance of anagnorisis, those of us with weak-minds are subjected, first, to feelings of horror;

then despair; then humility. And yet, finally, after scanning all possible cures and options, we experience a sorrowful acceptance of our fate—somewhat leavened, it is true, by a secret inner spurt of rejoicing, like a bright fountain concealed deep within the inspissate gloom of an obligatory socialized guilt.[4]

So far, the testimony of my eccentrics seems trivial compared to those more grandiose specimens I have named. Even so, the testimony of everyone is germane to the subject of bookish lunacies, for in one way or other, all of those rhapsodists are out of step with that real world which the majority know or think they know. All of those infatuates are members of a grand tribe of idiosyncratics who in their very divergence from assumed norms help define the human condition.

As an anecdotalist, I am pleased to contemplate their existence and the peculiar forms of their witnessing, for they all in their own ways reveal some part of the human condition, no matter how small or obscure that part is. It is possible to think of them as heroic in the way of pioneers and claim jumpers. Unlike the majority of people, who are either frantically trying to keep all the loud machines running or else snore their lives away in the proprieties of the moment, those pathfinders are out there in the darkness driving stakes in the *terra incognita* of the Past.

They are exploring some terrain that has never been adequately mapped, and, indeed, may never be. When you consider that most of the Past is utterly beyond recall, how can anyone resist the lure of visiting that small part of it which remains? Judged by one standard, at least, those bookish travelers are more alive than an entire drudge of corporation executives or a whole carnival of institutionalized celebrities. You know this is so because of the fact that

---

[4] Weak minds often given way to such rhetorical excess.

their faces will never appear on the cover of *Time* or *Newsweek*.

Such ruminations inspire me to recount one of the oddest conversations I have ever had. Indeed, it was so strange that I feel priviliged in having been part of it—playing straight man, as it were. This was at the AAUW used book sale held annually at the Methodist church in Granville—a small city in east-central Ohio and the home of Denison University. It was a cold and blustery April day, and I was standing near the front of a long line of people, underdressed and shivering, as I waited for the sale to begin, when I looked up to see my old friend, Powell Norris approaching.

Powell was large in every way—physically, as well as in his dealing and collecting, for he was prodigiously acquisitive and had many years before shown me a large oil portrait of Geronimo in his German Village warehouse in South Columbus. This old frame warehouse was badly in need of painting, and was as extravagant as its owner; it consisted of a converted six-car garage, with six pull-up doors and stalls designed for the narrow cars of the 1920s. There were no walls dividing the stalls and Powell had stuffed the entire building with an almost unbelievable accumulation of well-over 100,000 books, along with paintings, statuary and odd pieces of furniture. Raising any of those six doors was to face a wall of end shelves that were crammed to bursting with old tomes, and aisles between the shelves that would seem to be impassable to my beefy friend. And yet, Powell always somehow managed to wriggle his bulk into them and with a struggle like that of squeezing a hand into a too-small glove, work his way clear to the back, where there were sanctuaries of space large enough for one to actually extend both arms and turn around.

Our encounter at the Granville sale was the first time we'd seen each other for a decade or longer, so after our initial exchange of greetings, I asked Powell if he still had the

Geronimo portrait, which he had shown me in one of those spaces at the back of his warehouse.

"Oh, no, " he said, "I sold that years ago."

I was disappointed to hear it, for I remembered asking him at the time to let me know if and when he ever decided to sell it. But since the transaction was over, there was no point in complaining. Instead, I asked if he still had an old coffin I'd remembered seeing there.

"I've never had a coffin there," he said.

"What are you talking about?" I said. "I *saw* it."

Powell shook his head. "No, I've never had a coffin in my warehouse."

"What are you trying to *tell* me?" I cried, more upset by his denial of this fact than by his selling Geronimo without telling me. "I *saw* it!"

Then Powell Norris said one of the strangest things I've ever heard. He said, "No, there's never been a coffin in my warehouse, but if there had been, it wouldn't have had Ed Pratt's body in it."

"What?"

"Ed Pratt. There used to be this story about how I had stolen his body from the morgue up in Mt. Vernon."

"What in the hell are you talking about?"

"Don't you know who Ed Pratt was?"

I told him I did. He'd belonged to one of the wealthiest, most prominent and influential families in central Ohio. *Everybody* had heard of the Pratts.

"It was just some crazy story some people were passing around," he grumbled.

"Let me get this straight," I recapitulated. "You say you don't have, and have never had, a coffin in your warehouse—even though I distinctly remember seeing it there. And then you also claim that if you *had* had a coffin in your warehouse, it would not have had Ed Pratt's body in it. Do I have that right?"

Powell looked at me curiously, but then nodded, "That's right. Shortly after he was killed in a car accident out in the country, they took his body into the city morgue, but when they looked for it the next morning, it had disappeared."

"Disappeared from the city morgue," I repeated.

He nodded.

"Well," I said, "so far as I'm concerned, you're entirely innocent, because I'm sure there wasn't a body in the coffin I saw in your warehouse."

"I've never had a coffin in my warehouse," he said.

Which was sort of where we'd started. The loop was closed. Then they fired the gun to open the sale, and I was not to see Powell Norris ever again, for he died a few years later. But even though I never saw him again, I'm sure that the one I didn't see was not somebody else.

And yet, before entirely closing the loop of this anecdote, I should point out that I am as obsessed with old and rare books as Powell Norris, so you are entitled to consider the possibility, at least, that the coffin at the heart of my little story did not exist anywhere but in my mind. It seems that Powell thought so . . . or pretended to, anyway.

Ideally, the topic of bookish lunacies would include all the classic victims of *bacillus librorum,* along with the symptomology of such grand and puissant biblio-omnivores as those previously mentioned, with the addition of de Bury, Cotton, Beckford, Lenox and Widener. And of course those four mighty aiches—Heber, Huntington, Houghton and Hoe—should be described, embellished by anecdote, each anecdote appended by the tonic chord of a moral.

There should be a special place for the Rev. Isaac Gosset, D.D., F.R.S., described by Frederic Rowland Marvin in singularly unsympathetic and unflattering terms, referring to him as "a grotesque and at the same time vain-glorious dwarf."[5] Gosset gathered a great collection of pulpit litera-

---

[5] *Excursions of a Book-lover,* Bost., 1910. P. 44.

ture and Greek and Roman classics long before there were multitudes of collectors in the modern sense, and was evidently a lovable and affable man. His death in 1812 inspired the writing and publishing of a "poem of some length and well worth reading."[6]

Gosset's bibliomania was typical: engrossing, passionate, inspired; indeed, he seems to have talked aloud to his books, rather than letting them speak to him in silence, as more conventional readers do. He did not gather his eccentricities from the collecting of books, however; rather, he carried them with him, fully developed, into his collecting, for he took up collecting somewhat late in life, after he married a very wealthy woman, who had fallen in love with him while listening to his sermons. Marvin recounts the following anecdote from Gosset's career as a preacher:

> When in the pulpit, in order to see his congregation, he was compelled to stand upon two hassocks; and it is related that upon one occasion, being somewhat warmed up in his discourse, he slipped from the hassocks and for several minutes was invisible, though the sermon went on without interruption.[7]

One can only admire the little fellow's concentration in falling from such a height without missing a beat in his sermonizing.

Athough there is no evidence that all of those people I've listed were certifiably mad, many would argue that they were at least *touched* by lunacy or they would not have collected so exuberantly, so obsessively, and so well; for a great collection of books is a grand achievement, and grand

[6] Ibid., p. 50.
[7] Ibid., p. 44.

achievements are not possible without a skewing of common sense and quotidian priorities.[8] In short, great collectors are likely to be peculiar, which is to say, obsessed or touched by some version of madness.

The scope and character of so much divergence from our stereotypes of normality are inexhaustible studies—so obviously inexhaustible that it would not be practical to enter upon them here and try to explicate their intricacies in the small space proper to this essay. It would take volumes to speak of so much passion expended upon so many volumes, and there is surely not volume enough for it here.

But I will glancingly refer to one venerable source, the ostensibly fictitious testimony given by the narrator of Eugene Field's *The Love Affairs of a Bibliomaniac.* In one passage, this genial septuagenarian reports on Gladstone, saying he was so mad a collector that he fell into the habit of entering a bookstore and with one grand sweep of his arm buying all the books in it. Though appearing in a fiction, this report itself is evidently not entirely without substance.[9]

In our dreams, we have all made that expansive gesture, gathering whole libraries in our embrace, enriching our shelves to proliferation and bursting. But Field's narrator claimed to have witnessed this phenomenon personally, and was so impressed that he decided that any politician who showed a greater passion for collecting books than votes deserved both.

All true, in its way . . . although that way may be tortuous. In fact it's possible that Field's narrator got carried

---

[8] For those afflicted with logic, I will admit that the argument is circular; but like many circular arguments, it's true anyway—it's truth is just not proved by the argument.

[9] Gladstone's great political antagonist was none other than Benjamin Disraeli, son of that Isaac whose malicious attack on bibliophiles was quoted earlier. It is pleasant to contemplate the possibility that these two facts might be connected.

away . . . which should not surprise us greatly, for he has shown a certain instability from the very first pages. "I started out to be a philosopher," he said. As if that's not bad enough, a few pages later he gets so heated in talking about book fever that he crosses over the boundaries of metaphor, and begins to think of it as a real fever, the sort that actually causes physical discomfort, pain and even hallucination.

He then becomes so infatuated that he speaks of hearing about specific courses of treatment, treating bibliomania in such a way that it makes you think of mumps or measles: "To make short of a long story," he wrote, "the medical faculty is nearly a unit upon the proposition that wherever suppressed bibliomania is suspected immediate steps should be taken to bring out the disease."

When this solemn pronouncement is followed by the report that a physician named Woodbury claims that book-madness can be aborted in the first phase, our suspicion that he is having his fun with us turns into a certainty. For one thing, Woodbury is identified as being from Ohio. But even if that didn't signify a humorous turn, we would surely catch on some ninety pages later, when the narrator tells about a miligram of *bacillus librorum* being injected into the femoral artery of a cat, causing the demented creature to devour the covers of its own especially coveted edition of Rabelais. This edifying anecdote is immediately spoiled, however, when we are told that at least one person argued that Rabelais was actually an old rat.

Edifying or not, we immediately recognize Field's anecdote. It is even a sub-genre, of sorts (which makes it "a sort of sorts"); it gives us information about the collecting habits of men of old. Beyond any question, they were majestic in their bookish lunacies. And yet, it is my thesis that the species of grand eccentrics has not entirely died out. Its members are still here, and you may encounter them if only you know where to look.

And where should one look? Well, in antiquarian

bookstores, of course; or in the memberships of Friends of the Library organizations. And at book auctions, book and antique shows, antique shops and malls, flea markets, junk stores, estate and yard sales . . . and in the several publications whose readerships are explicitly and densely bookish.

You will not, of course, recognize them according to the stereotype of a bent and bearded old man shuffling in his slippers among the prized volumes of his library, ensconced away from an indifferent world of mindless noise. They will be young women with long dresses and long hair, and fat women in shorts, holding onto the hand of bewildered children; they will be bearded men in overalls and bespectacled men wearing neatly pressed suits and sharp-toed shoes. They will be students, lawyers, electricians . . . even politicians, like the late Maynard Sensenbrenner, Mayor of Columbus, Ohio, who years ago—even as the chief officer of a very large midwestern city—liked to haunt Salvation Army stores, looking for bargains among their accumulations of books. All variety of people, in short; but all possessed of uniquely furnished minds.

Finally, it must be admitted that this essay I am about to end is not the account of an outsider, or some sort of disinterested—much less, *uninterested* witness. The subject is not something remote I have travelled to, as a foreign correspondent might travel to Nepal or Uganda; for I myself am a member of that exotic population under scrutiny. Even though I am not aware of possessing any of its more spectacular and grandiose singularities, I am nevertheless something of an antiquarian—which is to say, one who is fascinated with the lives, deeds, habits and beliefs of people long dead.

In any popular view, that in itself is a certificate of eccentricity, if not madness. I do not have to sport a corduroy jacket over my raincoat in a downpour or speak of the dense clutter in an empty room or protest that a coffin that never existed did not contain a specific corpse to prove my membership. Simply devoting so many of my hours to the artifacts of the long dead is all that is required, and it is something I do willingly and with ineffable pleasure. Old disenfranchised realities show how fragile, and how pathetic and evanescent, all the passions of the moment will eventually prove to be. This is true of all moments, those of every time and every generation. It is, of course, one of the few absolute truths we know.

But what alternative is there to our imprisonment in the present moment? The Past is always there, and it's always interesting and always changing. We learn more and more about it, and are nourished by what we learn. It is, appropriately, antiquarian wisdom that the Past is an essential human dimension, and to ignore it utterly is a terrible evasion.

If books, as interior instruments, can seem to unfit us for the reality of the moment, such a sacrifice of "relevance" is a price some sensible people are willing to pay . . . even if other sensible people, those who are malignly unafflicted, cannot understand why they should pay anything at all, or what they are getting for their money.

12

Last Words

*T*here is a very small class of books devoted to the dying words of famous people. I have owned perhaps half a dozen copies of such anthologies during my years of active collecting, and have looked into perhaps twice that many. I have always read in them, if not, indeed, read any in their entirety; but they were probably never meant to be read straight through, in which case I haven't missed much. And yet, most have a peculiar fascination, one that is not in any way morbid. The last words of famous people are exit lines in the most theatrical moment of all: their departure from the drama of life.

Such a view is not without problems. Theater is essentially play, but dying is one of the most serious and least playful things we can do. In *Homo Ludens,* Johan Huizinga defined it as that which is circumscribed by time. It is activity that is "not for keeps," as small boys used to say when they played marbles with the understanding that all the marbles they'd "won" would be returned to their original owners after the game was over.

It has been generally and hopefully assumed by Europeans during most of the past five hundred years that there is a life after death, a mystical realm beyond the grave; and its character is determined by the quality of one's life. Given this world-view, the last words of a dying man or woman—especially one who was famous or noteworthy—carried an uncommon emphasis, being charged with vastly more meaning than those quotidian utterances locked into simply staying alive and getting from one day to the next.

So for centuries dying has been an eschatological drama, with the chief actor's exit lines inspired by God or perhaps a subsidiary divinity or influence. It was as if the words spoken were no longer rooted in the world of shovels, boots, and head colds, but were wafted upon ethereal gusts, whereof we have no understanding through the senses, but only through spiritual means. What the dying had to say was conclusive in the absolute sense, and at the same time might convey some form of witnessing of the World Beyond.

All of this explains why such books are not better known. They tend to be stultifying—inspirational, pious and edifying. They are so vapid as to turn believers into Atheists, if God is judged responsible for them. At a considerable saving of production costs, they could have been condensed into a broadside in the form of a petition or public declaration, with variations upon "I AM AT PEACE WITH GOD" printed at the top, followed by the names of all the deceased whose dying utterances fit the slogan.

Such inanities were not confined to the religious, however, Secular writers could also depart with banality. "I have had a happy life," William Hazlitt said immediately before he died; and the second question an impatient modern reader might ask is, "So what?" The first question is "Who was Hazlitt?" (The two questions are not, of course, entirely unrelated.)

Nevertheless, poor Hazlitt, unjustly neglected as a critic and essayist, should not be despised. People die of different afflictions, and not all are equally conducive to eloquence. Therefore, his dying utterance should not be seen as a measure of Hazlitt's abilities, for he wrote well and effectively, "leaving his mark on history," as people used to say, when they believed in history.

Although anthologies of dying words achieved their

greatest popularity in the 19th and early 20th century, they are still published. But today they tend to be frivolous and sensationalistic, somewhat like that related mini-class of books devoted to grotesque, sacrilegious, or just plain funny epitaphs. Recent anthologies tend to feature modern celebrities whose dying utterances were understandably unavailable to earlier anthologists.

Errol Flynn, whose career as a movie actor and womanizer made him both famous and infamous, departed from life muttering: "Hell, dying isn't so much!" Not bad at all, even though Flynn was hardly possessed of unimpeachable authority in saying so, since he hadn't quite done it yet. Still, it was very much type-casting for a leading man sort, and Hollywood could hardly have written it better. And it's not at all dispiriting, as were the last words of Max Baer—a jolly clown, a bit actor in Hollywood, and, before that, heavyweight boxing champion of the world. At the last moment, he cried: "Oh, God, here I go!"

Those slangy quotations would not have made the hit list of bygone anthologies, whose editors probably wouldn't have considered Errol Flynn and Max Baer worthy of quotation even if one of them had expired, saying, "I have made my peace with God and am content." What those old editors wanted was piety, by God, and that is what they got! But for most modern readers, those holy departures are so depressingly dull, it's a wonder some of the loved ones gathered around the bed weren't carried off, too.

Albrecht Von Haller, a Swiss physician and polymath, did it differently, however. He died in high style in 1777. He had been a child prodigy who at the age of four liked to read aloud from the Bible and expound upon the text before his father's no-doubt helpless servants. By the age of ten, he had "sketched a Chaldee grammar, prepared a Greek and Hebrew vocabulary, compiled a collection of two thousand biographies of famous men and women on the model of the great works of Bayle and Moreri, and written in Latin verses a satire on his tutor, who had warned him against a too great excursiveness [!]"[1]

There is much more, but you get the idea. And that business about the tutor suggests the possibility, at least, that young Haller may have been something of a monster. But the evidence is slight, and hardly damning, for it might have been all in fun, or the tutor might have deserved far worse. Not only that, whatever Haller may have been as a boy, he was apparently domesticated almost to the pitch of sainthood when he died, for his exit line from the drama of life is, in its gentle way, most interesting. Attended by a medical student (one must remember that the apprentice system prevailed in medicine, then, as in other dark arts), Haller put his fingers upon his own wrist at the base of the thumb and said, "And now, my friend, the pulse ceases to beat." Whereupon, he expired.

Human testimony being what it is, it's only natural that there are doubtful and incompatible reports of what a famous person actually said last. For example, what were Oscar Wilde's last words? One version has him looking at the new curtains on his window and saying "Either they go or I do." Spectacular flair, with a tinge of bitchiness that makes it seem too much like something Oscar had invented six months before. But his other famous last utterance was, "I am dying as I have lived—beyond my means." This is also good, and one has to acknowledge that he could have managed to say both shortly before he died; and yet, for the purist, only one dying utterance is allowed per person—the penultimate doesn't count. So we'll probably never know which exit line was the real one.

Although, if the agnostic Voltaire could repent on his death bed, might not Wilde have weakened in the face of that Final Darkness, where means and curtains are indistinguishable, and said something like "God forgive my sins!"

---

[1] *Encycl. Brit.,* 11th ed., p. 855.

No, this would be too much to contemplate; it just doesn't sound like him. So it must have been one of those exit lines quoted; and I think I'd put my money on the "beyond-my-means" bit, because I've seen more references to it than to the other . . . which isn't much of a reason, although it does suggest something like democracy at work in the editing of the past.

Like historical records, generally, reports of the dying words of the famous are often based upon surmise and later found to be inaccurate. And yet, this uncertainty doesn't make them less memorable. Consider poor old Tolstoy, passing away in the train station at Astapovo: "But the peasants . . ." he gasped, "how do they die?" Then there is Mme. Maurice Dupin, the mother of George Sand; woman-like (I speak of those older times), she said, "Please tidy my hair." A similar *amour propre* was even more touchingly evident in the last words of Bonnie Brown Hardy as she settled herself in the electric chair and asked, "Is my dress pulled down?"

That people do seem to carry themselves to their very ends is an odd and interesting feature of dying. Evidently, we are what we are as long as we are, the hope for celestial transformation notwithstanding. Consider Lord Chief Justice Tenterden, the son of a wigmaker, who achieved prominence in the law and, as a tory, was generally opposed to reform. As he lay dying in 1832, he fancied there was an entire jury seated before him. "Gentlemen," he said, "you are dismissed"; whereupon, he followed suit.

Heine died with his wit intact, along with a dash of impudence. Asked if he thought God would forgive his sins, he answered in French: "But of course he will; that's his business!" Surpassing this in impudence, but with a folksy, down-home style, was Cherokee Bill's answer when the sheriff asked if he had any last words before he was to be executed at the end of a rope: "Didn't come here to make a speech," Cherokee Bill said. "Come here to git *hung* ."

Old grudges, like professional habits, last on. The philosopher Hegel died muttering what could pass as a throwaway line from an old Groucho Marx movie: "Only one man ever understood me. And he didn't understand me." Leigh Hunt, a contemporary of Hazlitt, also exited with what sounds dangerously like a gag to modern ears: "I don't think I shall ever get over this." But for all the glory in these, I have yet to come upon the last words of an insomniac, saying, "I'm dying for a good night's sleep."

More gracious dispositions last on as well; and when Emily Dickinson died in 1886, she departed sounding wonderfully true to herself, gasping, "I must go in, the fog is rising." This could almost stand as a first line for one of her poems—one that might go something like this:

> I must go in—the fog is rising—
> so damp is earth's dear breath—
> might one catch cold from such a dew
> and breathing bring on death?

Indeed, it is remarkable how old habits last to the very end. Somewhere in the process, you would think, people would relinquish themselves, remove the *persona* of self and let some profounder latent truth, or abiding self, reveal itself. But most of the dying stubbornly remain themselves, dressed in all their old familiar habits. After all, themselves are all they've ever been; and old proprieties soothe them even when one might think they should be past caring; and old courtesies remain. Suicides who throw themselves off high bridges often remove their shoes. Under the circumstances, such a small gesture is not quite rational and strange to contemplate. It is not undiluted folly, however, for there is something like a stubborn dignity in it.

While I do not know Ian Fleming's last words, I do remember reading that shortly after he'd suffered the coronary that would kill him, he apologized to those on the emergency squad for being the cause of so much trouble.

This is a sad and whimsical ending for the creator of James Bond; and whatever it was he said, or how he said it, I suspect that neither Sean Connery nor Roger Moore could speak the lines as well on film as he did in fact.

And yet, there are inscrutable farewells whose wording seems either too deep for contemplation or might well have been changed had their speakers been more lucid. It all depends upon how you look at them. Some people, of course, are tempted to see mystical truth in such utterances, and palpate them for Delphic substance. Perhaps in these cases the mask of self has been removed, and that which is unsuccessfully articulated is indeed ineffable, and not easily accommodated to earthly diction and syntax.

Those who think this way are the inheritors of the voice-beyond-the-grave tradition—the "I have just glimpsed Eternity and have something to tell you" school. Subscribers to this creed believe that the dying are given to mystic utterance, and the language of mystics is not that of the media or market place. Consider Tennyson's departing, "I have opened it." What an antecedent looms somewhere there behind the pronoun *it* to tease the mind! Then, too, there is Goethe's ever-popular, "Licht, mehr Licht!"

One of the problems that vexes us is the realization that, when one is poised upon that last momentous transition, the truths and fictions of mortal existence blur until they are almost indistinguishable from one another. This is especially a problem if the one dying happens to be a fiction writer. One of the most wonderful last gasps was that attributed to Balzac, here quoted from V.S. Pritchett's biography of the great man (New York, 1973).

> Peritonitis, kidney trouble, started. The body filled with water. Finally, gangrene set in. Unable now to grasp anything, Balzac looked at his old friend Dr. Nacquart, who knew that the case was hopeless, and said to him suddenly, "Send for Bianchon'—the doctor he had invented in La Comedie Humaine.

But, alas, Pritchett's next sentence detracts from that perfect scene, for he writes: "This remark has been disputed." And yet, fiction writers will be tempted to let them dispute away, for the melodrama is too good to ignore. What is the claim of truth against such rhetoric? If Balzac hadn't been in such terrible shape for a dying man, one might be tempted to believe he was having a last little joke on reality—perhaps in the spirit of Wilde. And yet, the suffering is too vividly present to entertain such a notion.

———

It will be noted that a disproportionate number of the dying utterances so far quoted are by writers. This is hardly surprising, and does not in the least detract from those of other sorts of famous people. After all, last words of historical figures are to be found in books; and these books have been produced by writers, who show a natural preference for words . . . if not always for other writers. But writers themselves, schooled in valedictorian rhetoric (or at least in stylish scene endings), can hardly refrain from making their departures eloquent. Indeed, it seems only fitting, in a way, that they who have lived by the word, should die by the word.

Not only that, writers are the only people who carry their media with them to their deathbeds, if not to the grave. It is true that actors are similarly word-bitten, but their most memorable utterances come from a script, after all; and when actors die with the flourish of a quotation, more than half of what they say belongs to the playwright whose natural child it is. As for others among the famous dead: one would hardly expect a Rembrandt's last utterance to be a gesture in which he added a dab of purple to a painting he was working on; or an Einstein to gasp out a last revolutionary new formula for humankind to contemplate. And if Bach died humming, he could have hardly managed the polyphony that glorifies his music.

No, deathbed utterances belong pretty much to the literati. These existential exit scenes appeal to the sense of drama that even a shy and retiring novelist must possess in at least some degree. Or poet. Wordsworth's last years were embittered by the death of his elder daughter, Dorothy, known as "Dora." When he lay on his deathbed, the eighty year old poet's wife, Mary, came to tell him he was dying. "William," she said to him, "you are going to Dora." When Mary's niece came to him the next morning, he asked, "Is that Dora?"

Though he was clearly (some might say "unclearly") a novelist, there is no evidence that the author of *Tristram Shandy* was shy and retiring; in fact, Laurence Sterne seems to have been an incorrigible and relentless wag. Thomas Gray wrote that, even while watching him read his sermons, ". . . you see him often tottering on the verge of laughter, and ready to throw his periwig in the face of his audience."

It's a pity that Sterne couldn't have saved a good one for the end; but such was not to be. In his biography of Sterne, Lewis Melville reports the scene as follows (the quoted parts are from John Macdonald's *Travels in Various Parts of Europe*):

> "I went to Mr. Sterne's lodging," Macdonald reported on his return; "the mistress opened the door; I enquired how he did. She told me to go up to the nurse; I went into the room, and he was just a-dying. I waited ten minutes; but in five he said, 'Now it is come!' He put off his hand as if to ward off a blow, and died in a minute.' Thus on March 18, 1868, passed away the most volatile and whimsical writer of his age.

Macdonald's report is not without interest, for we see poor befuddled dying Sterne waiting ten minutes for a death that happens in six. But that is a minor muddlement, and has nothing nearly so grand about it, in the way of temporal confusion, as Melville's sentence that has the novelist dying on the right day, and in the right month, although exactly one century too late.

Over a real century later, on the other side of the Atlantic, a lesser but more famous writer died with equal clarity. I refer to Harriet Beecher Stowe as she lay on her deathbed the last morning of her life and watched the approach of her nurse bearing medicine. In her eighty-sixth year, the author of *Uncle Tom's Cabin* had been interestingly peculiar for several years, giving her neighbors in Hartford, Connecticut, a lot to talk about and forgive. But now she rose to the occasion long enough to make a single lucid statement, although it's not clear to whom she spoke. "I love you," she said, then died.

Although it is easy for us to forget what a great writer John Galsworthy was to his contemporaries, there are rumblings of recrudescence in the direction of his reputation; and perhaps the day may come when he will take his place in the role of masters of fiction. Not too long ago, *The Forsyte Saga* was given handsome treatment in a television series, and Galsworthy's beautiful short story, "Quality," still finds its way into anthologies upon occasion. Therefore, his last words are fitting to be quoted, but I will use George Sims' description of the death-bed scene:

> "Brigagen ... abrigagen . . . brabigen ... jump ... Spring . . . goodbye, goodbye, goodbye . . . . " With broken utterances such as these and bouts of speech-lessness and a hostile glare for the world which had laden him with riches and honours, the distinguished author John Galsworthy died. A number of eminent surgeons, doctors and specialists had clustered about his bedside, as in Shaw's *The Doctor's Dilemma,* but they had been unable to decide whether he was suffering from a brain tumour, or some secondary growth or virulant anaemia. The diagnosis of a brain

tumour was never confirmed by a post mortem and it is possible that his trouble may have been some fatal malaise of the spirit. "Something evil and final . . ." as his G.P., Dr. J.W. Darling, put it in a letter to Galsworthy's nephew Rudolph Sauter some eight days before the great man's death.[2]

I find all of this quite mysterious—Sims' and Dr. Darling's contributions, as well as Galsworthy's enigmatic farewell. What do those first three words mean? I'm not even sure how to pronounce them, although I would assume that the *g* s are soft before *e* ; still, where does that leave us? All one can say is that, while Galsworthy may have written a most conservative prose, his exit lines were more appropriate to his contemporary, Joyce.

And what *about* Joyce? While his last words are not identified as such in Richard Ellmann's massive biography, there are several interesting approximations. On January 8, 1941, while dining at the Kronenhalle in Zurich, "he remarked casually to Frau Zumstag, over a bottle of Mont Benet, 'Perhaps I won't be here much longer.'"

A few days later he collapsed and was operated on for a perforated duodenal ulcer. Regaining consciousness, he was told that he'd gotten blood transfusions from two Swiss soldiers from Neuchatel, and replied, "A good omen; I like Neuchatel wine." But then he lapsed into a coma, and shortly after midnight on January 13, he regained consciousness only long enough to ask for his wife and son, then fell into a coma once again and died. Ellmann does not say whether his request to see his wife and son was his last utterance, but if it was, and if it was properly and clearly enunciated, there is a certain felicity in the fact, for Joyce was as conservatively bourgeois in his personal life as he was bohemian in his art . . . thus making a perfect complement to

---

[2] *More of The Rare Book Game,* Phila., 1988. p. 79.

the artistically conservative Galsworthy, who, when his candle burnt low, went out sputtering like an Earwick.

But what reference to the last words of great writers would be complete without Anton Chekhov's valedictory? I take this from what may seem an unlikely source, Lydia Avilov's *Checkhov in My Life*—a book written by the great man's mistress, translated and with an Introduction by David Magarshack. This is an interesting and curious book, with the last paragraph of the Introduction largely devoted to Chekhov's wife's account of his death, as follows:

> "He woke up in the early hours of the morning," his wife writes, "and for the first time asked me to send for the doctor. When the doctor came, he ordered some champagne for him. Chekhov sat up and said to the doctor in German in a loud and rather significant voice, 'Ich sterbe.' Then he took the glass, turned his face to me, and with his wonderful smile said, 'It is a long time since I drank champagne . . . ' He then quietly drank his champagne, lay down on his left side, and soon grew silent forever . . . "

We can only hope that the champagne was a good year.

If writers have so often proved reliable in seizing the opportunity for high drama in their departure from life, what could be more natural than their letting the creatures of their imagination depart with similar dignity? We have already met Balzac's Dr. Bianchon, and know that the characters created by a novelist can be more real to the imagination than actual people, equipped with all the confusions of authenticity.

But here the focus is not upon a writer's own last words, but upon the last words and gestures of the creatures he has created. One of the grandest and most melodramatic exits, in or out of fiction, is that of the Chicago gangster

Rico, in W.R. Burnett's *Little Caesar.* You will remember
that he has finally been gunned down in a dark alley by "a
big man in a derby hat." In the film, Rico's nemesis is the
detective, Flaherty, who has vowed to get him and take him
in, with handcuffs on his wrists. Rico is, of course, played
by Edward G. Robinson, in perhaps his most famous role.
(It is said that when Robinson had occasion to visit
Chicago, shortly after the movie came out, the local
gangstabulary practically queued up to meet him—simply
one more example of how life imitates art.)

As the film Rico lies dying, he looks up at Flaherty and
tells him that he still won't be taken in handcuffed. Then he
asks, "Is this the end of Rico?" and dies. It's a wonderful
scene, played excellently by Robinson; but, while different
from the way Burnett wrote it in the novel, it is no better. For
this is how he dies in the novel: "'Mother of God,' he said,
'is this the end of Rico?'" A slight variation, to be sure; but
an important one—no doubt bowdlerized in the manner of
the time, for the Hays Office did not take to gratuitous appeals to the deity any more than to the inside of a woman's
thigh. And, while in the film the Contest motif is closed by
Flaherty's obvious victory, the novel ends with far less clarity, and far more mystery. We are not told exactly who "the
big man in the derby hat" is, which in narrative terms is a far
more powerful ending than that of the film . . . as good as
that is for its quite different cinematic purposes.

When thinking of fictional deaths, however, who will
ever forget Popeye's grim demise in *Sanctuary*? Faulkner's
gothic imagination has never worked better than in pictur-
ing his demonic creature's final moment on the scaffold,
when he interrupts the preacher's prayer.

> Popeye began to jerk his neck forward in little jerks.
> "Psssst!" he said, the sound cutting sharp into the
> drone of the minister's voice; "pssssst!" The sheriff
> looked at him; he quit jerking his neck and stood

rigid, as though he had an egg balanced on his head. "Fix my hair, Jack," he said. "Sure," the sheriff said. "I'll fix it for you"; springing the trap.

Whatever the status of actuality or art in Balzac's own demise, in his fiction he beyond doubt created one of the classical exit scenes. The melodrama is gorgeous, over-stated, powerful, comical in its excess—and a little bit eerie. My reference is to the deathbed gesture of Eugenie Grandet, eponym of one of Balzac's greatest novels, and a creature of demonic cupidity and greed. Indeed, he has lived his whole life so rapacious for wealth that it seems as inevitable as it is shocking that when he is lying in his death bed, and a priest enters in order to administer the last rites—leaning over the dying man, his golden crucifix swinging on its chain before him—that old Grandet seeing it glittering before his fading eyes, with his last energy lifts his hand and *gropes* for it!

Socrates was hardly a fictional character, even if Plato did at times seem to be writing about a different man from the one featured in Xenophon's *Memorabilia*. The great philosopher's last words are, of course, among the most fa-mous ever recorded. To his friend Crito he said: "We owe a cock to Asklepios; pay it and do not forget." But the full meaning behind this charge is perhaps not so well known; a sacrifice to the god of medicine was customary for those who had just recovered from an illness, so that Socrates' implied meaning seems to be that in dying he will recover from the illness of life itself.

The taint of *Weltschmerz* in Socrates' last utterance might seem more appropriate to someone like Mark Twain; and yet—misanthrope that he was—he took pity at the last moment, and restrained himself from delivering what might have been expected in the way of an excoriation against The Damned Human Race—or, if not that, perhaps some tumble of drollery that would leave them rolling in the aisles. According to Albert Bigelow Paine in his four-volume biography, Twain's dying words were not words at all, but only a single word (though sometime compounded): "Goodbye."

That is gratifyingly sensible, certainly; but for nobility, you have to go to Twain's foil and contemporary, Henry James, who is reported to have said, immediately before dying: "Ah, here it is, the Distinguished Thing!" I add the capital letters, aware that he could hardly have *spoken* those words as such; but I include them anyway, for they have the right feel. James' utterance has grand style, not to mention a dash of bravery. It's far better than you might expect from a man whom Stephen Crane described as "an effeminate old donkey"; but then, Crane was a baseball player, among other things, and he met James when the old master's pained fastidiousness in conversation—what Edith Wharton called his "elaborate hesitancies"—were likely to have a disagreeable effect upon just about anyone who had to listen to him grope his way toward the next semi-colon, with not a period in sight.

Along with most of the other star performers quoted, James and Twain seemed to have known very well that they were dying, which suggests either that the imminence of death provides an unmistakably unique sensation or that the theatrical power of a last utterance can function as a self-fulfilling prophecy for those who are on the brink, as they say . . . or, perhaps, a little of both.

Given the fact that deathbed rhetoric tends toward high drama, and even melodrama, it is only appropriate that actors should be remembered. All who knew her, or who had seen her act, agreed that Charlotte Cushman, perhaps America's most famous Lady Macbeth in the 19th century, was a woman of great and commanding presence.

She was also a woman of strong conviction, and argued that in all the major scenes of the "Scottish play" all the major characters were supposed to be drunk. She was convinced that this was Shakespeare's intention, and claimed that the text not only supported such a theory, but insisted upon it. She died in 1876, and was remarkably lucid until the end. Having asked to have Lowell's "Columbus" read to her, she supplied the missing words with perfect confidence and accuracy whenever the reader hesitated.

Of the many great and famous statesmen who have departed with a memorable utterance or an eloquent gesture, George Washington is notable and particularly relevant to the present context. According to Noemie Emery, in her *Washington: A Biography* (New York, 1976), the great man's last words were not in themselves memorable; he simply muttered, "'Tis well." But then, Emery writes the following, which is most apt in the present context:

> These were his last words. Shortly before eleven his breathing eased. "He lay quietly," Lear [his secretary] wrote, "withdrew his hand from mine & felt his own pulse—I spoke with Dr. Craik who sat by the fire—he came to the bedside—the General's hand fell from his wrist . . . Dr. Craik put his hand on his eyes and he expired without a struggle or a sigh.

So it is that with that touching gesture we have come back full cycle to that other good and great man, Albrecht Von Haller. Dying has its conventions, after all—there are fads and fashions in our final departures; how could there not be, since it is a human event? Near the end of the 18th century it might have been customary for a person of substance, when dying, to reach for his or her own pulse, to savor entirely the finality of expiring.

Today, of course, we don't have to resort to such crude methods, for there are instruments to indicate the fact. And yet, such instruments do not entirely deprive us of some of our comfortable old human problems, for though the fact of death seems absolute and final, the actual moment of death is not always certain. A clear definition is not easy to come by, because the vital organs are not synchronized in their cessation.

It has been said that the only sure sign is bodily decay. But that seems like waffling, because who can say when the decay begins? Or how can it be identified as it happens, in the event, rather than by its symptoms? Decay is hardly more of an absolute than the disappearance of a detectable respiration or pulse. Not only that, is gangrene in the foot sufficient cause to put an otherwise living body in the ground? Hardly. Only the foot, one would suppose; and, indeed, I once knew a man whose foot was buried, but I doubt if it said anything memorable before dying.

Still, the decay test is not without merit. And after general decomposition has advanced far enough, there can be little doubt remaining . . . for a rational creature, at least. Therefore, if we wanted to agonize over the question of when life ends as so many agonize over when it begins, we could depend upon decay to provide an especially cogent argument when combined with the corroboration afforded by instrumental witnessing.

No doubt there's something like comfort in this. However, what long-range effect electronic monitors might have upon last words is beyond the range of speculation at this time. But it seems likely that death will always be accomplished pretty much in the same old, time-tested way; and the star performer's last utterances will continue to interest and amuse a great many people, even if the day when anthologies of deathbed rhetoric flourished has passed.